Relationship Anxiety

7 Steps to Freedom from Jealousy, Attachment, Worry, and Fear – Heal and Rediscover Your Love for Each Other

Relationship Anxiety

acknowledge that the author is not engaged in the rendering of legal, financial, medical or professional advice. The content within this book has been derived from various sources. Please consult a licensed professional before attempting any techniques outlined in this book.

By reading this document, the reader agrees that under no circumstances is the author responsible for any losses, direct or indirect, that are incurred as a result of the use of the information contained within this document, including, but not limited to, errors, omissions, or inaccuracies.

Table of Contents

Your Free Gift

As a way of saying thanks for your purchase, I want to offer you a free bonus e-Book called *7 Essential Mindfulness Habits* exclusive to the readers of this book.

To get instant access, just go to:

https://theartofmastery.com/mindfulness

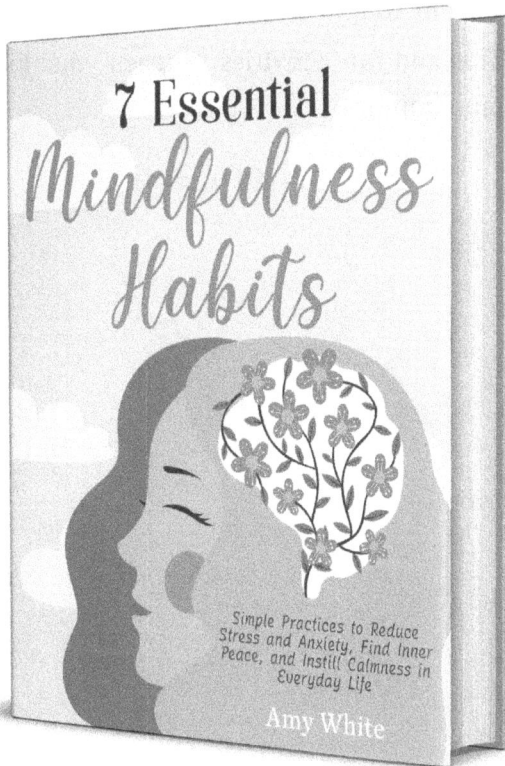

Inside the book, you will discover:

- What is mindfulness meditation?
- Why mindfulness is so effective in reducing stress and increasing joy, composure, and serenity
- Various mindfulness techniques that you can do anytime, anywhere
- 7 essential mindfulness habits to implement starting today
- Tips and fun activities to teach your kids to be more mindful

Introduction

"Your task is not to seek love, but merely to seek and find all the barriers within yourself that you have built against it."

~ Rumi

Do you fear being rejected or abandoned? Do you spend nights worrying that your partner doesn't feel the same way about you? Are you afraid of commitment? Do you feel as if your relationship inflames your struggles instead of soothing them? What you are dealing with is relationship anxiety, and it has weakened the connection and stolen the magic between you and your significant other. Even though healthcare professionals are aware of this type of anxiety, it has not been recognized by the Diagnostic and Statistical Manual of Mental Health. Unlike other forms of anxiety, like panic disorder and generalized anxiety disorder, doctors are unable to provide specific guidelines for a diagnosis or treat relationship anxiety. But with an estimated one in five people suffering from the condition, experts are paying close attention to it and providing effective strategies for couples to overcome it.

I suffered from relationship anxiety for years before I found out it existed. I spent my life jumping in and out of relationships because I self-sabotaged the majority of them. Some of my boyfriends just got so fed up with my accusations and insecurities, they would leave. When I got married, I thought to myself, *Finally, someone accepts me for me* because I actually believed that my behavior was normal. I assumed it was just the way I was until my husband filed for a divorce. He hoped he could change me, but after years of trying, he got tired and left.

I still didn't get it; I was in complete denial that there was something wrong. I didn't even consider it. I kept repeating the same patterns and got married again, but this time, I married someone exactly like me. We both suffered from relationship anxiety, and it wasn't long before we were desperately miserable. We wanted the marriage to last and decided to go to marriage counseling. It was here that we found freedom; our counselor labeled our issues as relationship anxiety and worked with us to overcome them.

Today, our relationship is strong, passionate, and fulfilling. Do we have problems? Yes, absolutely. But we now know how to resolve them without resorting to the silent treatment or a screaming match. I am not trying to sell you the secrets to a perfect relationship because it doesn't exist. Humans are complex beings, and it takes patience and commitment for couples to get to the point where they understand each other. But what I do know is that relationship anxiety can sabotage your union if you don't overcome it. In this book, you can expect:

- To learn about relationship anxiety symptoms
- Attachment theory and the root cause of your relationship anxiety
- How to resolve conflict in your relationship
- How to keep the passion alive in your relationship

Humans were not created to live alone, and neither were we created to be miserable in the relationship we are in. There is an overwhelming number of mental and physical consequences associated with being in an unhealthy relationship. Studies have found that toxic relationships increase your risk of developing a heart condition. Hostile relationships can delay healing, and the high stress levels can weaken the immune system and cause organ damage. Additionally, an unhealthy relationship can cause depression, personality disorders, and extreme anxiety.

When you learn how to manage relationship anxiety, you will experience what I have termed the "paired figure skating effect," where you are gliding effortlessly in relationship bliss and no matter which position you are in, whether holding hands or on the other side of the skating rink, you remain in sync and connected because you are moving to the same choreographed routine.

If you are struggling with relationship anxiety, don't make the same mistake as I did for years, and get comfortable with your fears. Make a commitment today to fight back against anxiety and follow these seven steps to freedom and the rediscovery of your love for each other.

Chapter 1: Relationship Anxiety – What is it?

"Anxiety does not empty tomorrow of its sorrows, but it empties today of its strength." ~ Charles Spurgeon

You've met the man or woman of your dreams; they are perfect in every way. You understand each other, you speak each other's love language, you trust each other, but something isn't quite right. You can't find peace with the relationship, and you have this terrible, gut-wrenching fear that it isn't going to last. You are constantly bombarded with negative thoughts about your significant other, and it's putting a strain on the relationship. According to experts, this is known as relationship anxiety. It's normal to have some anxiety in a relationship, especially during the beginning stages; however, when you get to the commitment stage, and these worries are still plaguing you, it can start having a negative effect on your life and cause the following:

- Emotional exhaustion or fatigue
- A lack of motivation
- Emotional distress
- Physical symptoms, such as constant stomachaches

In many cases, relationship anxiety has nothing to do with the actual relationship. The problem often stems from childhood trauma that you haven't resolved.

Signs of Relationship Anxiety

Relationship anxiety can show up in different ways depending on the unique circumstances of your partnership. However, there are some common traits, and this is what they look like:

Sabotage: Deep-seated insecurity that you may or may not be aware of leads people to push loved ones away. Subconsciously, they don't believe they deserve love and will do things like pick arguments, test boundaries, and refuse to communicate. You may also feel that you need to test your partner to see if they really love you. As far as you are concerned, if you pull every trick in the book to get them to leave and they stay, it is interpreted as their devotion to you. Again, this is not something you do consciously (we will get into that in Chapter 2).

Do I Matter? This is a common manifestation of relationship anxiety. It reveals itself as an unhealthy desire to know whether you matter to your partner. Is your partner really concerned about making sure you feel secure? According to family and relationship expert Tia Robinson, this stems from the need to feel a sense of belonging and connection in the relationship. You spend a lot of time worrying about things like:

- Whether they would stick around if something serious happened to you.
- How much your partner misses you when you are not around.
- Whether they are only with you because of what you bring to the table.

Do They Want to End it? When you feel happy, secure, and loved in your relationship, it's perfectly normal to want to keep things this way. However, obsessing over it isn't. When you are constantly looking for signs to confirm that your partner wants to end the relationship, you trap yourself in a prison of self-inflicted fear. This becomes a problem when you start changing your behavior in hopes that your loved one doesn't leave. You might do things like:

- Stay silent about boundaries that are being broken
- Do things you don't enjoy doing just to please your partner
- You say yes to their every request, so you don't upset them

Afraid They Don't Really Love You: You've both said "I love you," and your partner not only tells you but shows you how they feel about you all the time. They do sweet things like cook you dinner and surprise you with flowers. But, when your partner doesn't text you back immediately, goes out without you, or doesn't spend every minute you are together hugging you, you start panicking that they don't love you. To some extent, these concerns are normal in a relationship, but it becomes a problem when you are consumed by them.

Always Questioning Things: There is nothing wrong with being inquisitive, but when you are always scrutinizing every move your partner makes, you are heading for disaster. With relationship anxiety, not only do you question your partner, you question yourself. Every move you make is carefully calculated, and making simple decisions can take days or weeks. Again, it is healthy to stand back and evaluate a situation before stepping into it. But when you become stuck in an endless cycle of self-doubt and worry, you can make life very difficult for yourself.

Afraid it Will Happen Again: If you've had negative experiences with relationships in the past, it can affect the way you view your current relationship. You are so afraid of getting hurt again that you either don't allow your partner to get too close, look for signs that they are the same as your ex, or subconsciously sabotage the relationship so that it ends before you get too attached. Learning to trust someone again after going through relationship trauma is difficult, and in most cases, you are not aware of the psychological triggers that cause you to act this way.

Why do You Feel Anxious in Your Relationship?

At its extreme, anxiety is a challenging mental health disorder which can cause many problems if it isn't resolved. Not only will it have a negative effect on you, but the manifestations of anxiety can also destroy your relationship. The intensity with which you display the symptoms above will determine whether you have reached the stage where it's time to start challenging your issues. You may also find that your anxiety is expressed physically through symptoms such as insomnia, shortness of breath, shaking, nausea, and panic attacks. These feelings are brought on whenever you start overthinking, and they are the physiological signs that you are suffering from an anxiety disorder.

Emotional intensity is the hallmark of an intimate relationship. When you share a deep connection with another person, that closeness can sometimes render you powerless, and it can leave you feeling insecure and anxious. Insecurity is a lack of self-confidence, and anxiety is fear of the unknown. Insecurity will turn into anxiety if it's not addressed. Additionally, constant worry about your relationship breeds low self-esteem and self-hatred. Your partner then becomes a target because everything they do is viewed through a negative lens.

As mentioned, anxiety is a fear of the future which means that in most cases, it's not your partner's behavior that's the problem, it's the imaginary thoughts that keep running around in your head. You are your biggest critic; we all have a negative inner voice that is always trying to prevent us from living our best lives. Your inner critic will tell you things like:

- *You are not smart, funny, or attractive enough, and so your partner will soon get bored of you.*
- *They are only pretending to love you. Dump them before they dump you.*
- *They are not to be trusted. You are just a fill-in until they find someone better.*
- *You are not good enough for someone to truly love you, so just don't bother.*

This evil voice in your head speaks so loudly and so often that it manages to convince you of everything that it's saying. The voice turns you against yourself and the person you love. It makes you hostile and paranoid, it destroys your self-esteem, and you become stressed, anxious, jealous, and defensive. Even if you have found the "one," if you keep listening to this voice, it will jeopardize your happiness, and you will find it difficult to enjoy your relationship. When your focus is on the wrong things, it becomes impossible to focus on the things that will enrich your relationship, and all your time and energy are spent in self-destruct mode.

For example, it's date night, and you and your partner have arranged to go and see a movie and go out to dinner. But at the last minute, they cancel because their mom fell down the stairs and broke her leg and gets rushed to the hospital. Instead of being sympathetic to your partner's mother's hardship, your main concern is whether he/she is lying so they can go and see their other lover. Your evening is spent thinking about all the worst-case scenarios. To make matters worse, you can't get through to your partner on the phone. Not because they are out cheating, but because, in general, hospitals don't have good phone reception. Your response is to bombard your partner with accusatory text and voice messages. When they leave the hospital, their phone starts blowing up, and after all the stress they've just been through dealing with their mother, the last thing they need is a fight.

The result? Your anxiety has successfully caused a problem that didn't need to be there. So when your partner starts distancing themselves from you (and they have every right to do so), you take it as confirmation that your fears were indeed correct, but the reality is that it was your behavior that caused the problem.

Using the above scenario as an example, why is it that some people take the cancellation as a sign of infidelity, and others will calmly accept that their partner had to tend to their mother, and they can reschedule at a later date? The answer lies in the root cause of many mental health conditions, and that is your attachment style.

Chapter 2: Your Attachment Style Will Determine the Quality of Your Relationship

"The quality of your life is the quality of your relationships." ~ Anthony Robbins

The notion of attachment became a psychological theory in 1958. It was developed by psychologist John Bowlby after he spent several years working in a psychiatric clinic for children in London. During his time at the clinic, he treated and cared for many children suffering from emotional disturbance. Due to behavioral patterns Bowlby observed in the children, he began to suspect that there was a correlation between the relationship they had with their mothers and their cognitive and emotional development. In particular, it shaped Bowlby's beliefs about maladjustment later on in life and early infant separation from mothers. It was these conclusions that led him to formulate the attachment theory.

According to Bowlby, attachment relates to the deep psychological connection between humans. He argued that attachment could be evaluated from an evolutionary context because the caregiver is responsible for providing security and safety for the child. The infants' chances of survival are dependent upon whether or not this attachment is formed in the right way. Bowlby suggests that it is a universal reaction for babies to desire the security of their mothers when they feel threatened or stressed. His research concludes that there are four main attachment styles formed during childhood, and they will determine the quality of your adult relationships.

Secure Attachment: David and Nicola are the prototypical cute couple. They call each other cute nicknames, they have a catalog of inside jokes, they say things at the same time, and from the outside looking in, they appear to have the perfect union. But the success of their relationship is not due to cuteness overload; it's because they both have a secure attachment style.

People with a secure attachment style are confident in who they are. They have confidence in their partner and in their relationship. They trust their partner enough to allow them to be independent. They know how to give and receive support and don't have a problem being vulnerable. And this is why David and Nicola have such a strong relationship. However, please understand that this doesn't mean they are perfect, and neither is their relationship. Life is never all sunshine and roses. There are going to be ups and downs, but because they both have a secure attachment style, they will work it out and become better as a result. A secure attachment is the foundation for a good relationship. The characteristics of people in a relationship with a secure attachment style include:

- **Trust:** Trust involves two people having enough confidence in each other that commitment becomes easy. The level of commitment deepens because building trust is practiced.

- **Good Conflict Resolution:** As mentioned, there is no such thing as a perfect relationship, and couples are going to have disagreements. However, it is how you resolve those arguments that will make or break your partnership. People with a secure attachment style know how to resolve conflict, and they will have a strategy in place to do so. For example, they won't raise their voices, they won't call each other names, and they won't play the blame game. Instead, they will calmly discuss the issue and make a point of listening to each other.

- **Security:** People in a secure relationship don't worry about the future. They are not concerned about where things are headed. They enjoy being present with one another and don't feel the need to put unnecessary demands on the relationship.

Their partnership is secure because they are secure in themselves.

- **Comfortable with Vulnerability:** A relationship won't survive without vulnerability. Both parties must be willing to express their hurts, fears, and emotions in order to build trust. Since people with a secure attachment style don't tend to have trust issues, they find it easy to open up when they are with the right person.

Anxious Attachment: People with an anxious attachment style experience consistent anxiety in their relationships. This attachment style develops when parents do not allow their children to express vulnerability, and neither are they sensitive to the emotional needs of the child. Adults with an anxious attachment style are very insecure and have difficulty trusting their partners. They will typically experience the following:

- **Fear of Abandonment:** People with an anxious attachment style don't feel secure in their relationships because they are afraid their partner will change their mind about them and leave. If you are constantly saying to your partner things like, "I know you're going to leave me at some point," or "I doubt this relationship is going to work," there is a high chance you are afraid of being abandoned.

- **Constant Attention-Seeking:** Attention-seeking is one of the many symptoms of the fear of abandonment. Someone who fears abandonment will do everything in their power to hold on to their relationship, and that includes making up stories to get their partner to feel sorry for them. Bombarding their significant other with text messages in hopes they will keep thinking about them, or excessive posting on social media.

- **The Need to be Taken Care Of:** People with an anxious attachment style want someone to look after them, and a romantic partner is often their main target. They feel better when they have someone fussing over them, and to get the attention they are looking for, they may engage in self-harm or self-destructive behaviors. People with an anxious attachment style are also known to feign sickness and are constantly going to the doctor for a diagnosis.

- **The Need for Validation:** Due to the fact that adults with an anxious attachment style didn't feel truly loved as children, they grow up seeking validation from others. This can come in the form of people-pleasing and always needing to hear they are appreciated and wanted by their partner.

Avoidant Attachment: Maybe it's the CEO who works 80-hour weeks and needs to be alone on the weekends. He will see you, but he has a strict schedule and will only make room for one date night a week. Or it's the woman who is always going on dates, meets some really nice guys, but never makes a commitment. These are characteristics of the avoidant attachment style. Whether directly or indirectly, avoiders will make it known that they are not going to be available when the topic of the Christmas holidays comes up with a romantic partner. They are the nitpickers in a relationship and will focus on the most insignificant things to distance themselves from the person they are dating. When the relationship ends (which is typically their choice), they regret it. People with an avoidant attachment style prefer doing things alone, but eventually, they realize they want intimacy; they just don't know how to maintain it. There are several personality traits that will determine whether a person has an avoidant attachment style. These include:

- **Sabotaging Relationships:** When they like the person they are dating, they have high hopes for the future. But when things start getting serious, they become fearful that their significant other will change their mind and leave. To avoid this, they start doing things to sabotage the relationship, like staying out all night when they know it upsets their partner. Or having flirtatious conversations on the phone in front of the person they are dating.

- **Resisting Vulnerability:** Vulnerability in a relationship means you've got to open up to your partner. People with an avoidant attachment style don't like expressing their emotions, and so vulnerability is something they struggle with.

- **Pulling Away:** When a person with an avoidant attachment style starts catching feelings, they will disappear. This will happen several times throughout the relationship. When emotions come to the surface, they run a mile and then show up when they think they've got their emotions under control.

- **Sexual but Not Emotional:** People with an avoidant attachment style are very comfortable having casual sexual relationships because they can avoid emotional commitment. If they are in a relationship, they are the type who will have sex with you and then go cold afterward. You can expect them to do things like jump out of bed after the deed, take a shower, and say they've got to go out. Or ask you to leave because their mother is coming over.

- **Shallow Relationships:** They will put great efforts into ensuring the relationship doesn't get any deeper than it needs to. The person on the other end finds themselves constantly trying to take things to the next level, but they get shut down every time.

Disorganized Attachment: This is the most extreme of the attachment styles. It is a combination of the avoidant and anxious attachment and typically develops in adults who were either physically, emotionally, or sexually abused as children. The disorganized attachment style is characterized by inner conflict, mistrust, and fear. When in relationships, their behavior is volatile and unpredictable, and they typically display the following traits:

- **Low Self-Esteem:** When a person has been abused as a child, the result is low self-esteem. They have been conditioned to believe they are unlovable. In a relationship, these feelings manifest in various ways, including self-sabotage, attention-seeking, and abandoning the relationship for no reason.

- **Aggressive Behavior:** People with a disorganized attachment don't know how to deal with stress. They find it difficult to regulate their emotions because they lack coping skills. Since they don't know how to cope with stress, they often resort to aggressive behavior. People with a disorganized attachment style are known to physically abuse their partners.

- **Fear of Rejection:** The fear of rejection manifests in several ways, but they all lead to one outcome: a self-fulfilling prophecy. As mentioned, a person with a disorganized attachment style suffers from very low self-esteem, so they don't believe they are worthy of love. They are always looking for confirmation of their fears, and that can include going through their partner's phone and private belongings. This constant suspicious behavior is what leads to the deterioration of the relationship. When it ends, their fear is confirmed, but the irony is that it was their behavior that pushed the person away.

- **Deep-Rooted Shame:** Toxic shame opens the door to self-disgust, anger, and other undesirable feelings. It involves constant negative self-evaluation that focuses on a person's identity. In general, people can acknowledge their mistakes, learn from them, and move on. This is not the case with people who suffer from shame. They will keep reminding themselves of the mistake and emotionally attach it to their identity. It prevents people from seeing themselves in a positive light because, deep down, they believe they are defective in some way.

Questionnaire to Discover Your Attachment Style

When you know your attachment style, you will find it a lot easier to overcome your relationship anxiety. The results from the questionnaire below will help you determine your attachment style. To answer the questions, give yourself a score from 1–5:

1 = Very true, 2 = Almost true, 3 = Slightly true, 4 = Majority false, 5 = Very false

1. I find it easy to establish an emotional connection with people.
2. I don't feel comfortable depending on other people.
3. I am concerned that my partner doesn't care about me in the same way I care about them.
4. I don't feel comfortable when my partner wants a committed relationship.

5. I don't feel complete when I'm not in a relationship.
6. I am always trying to resolve other people's issues.
7. I let my partner make all the decisions.
8. I do everything my partner tells me to.
9. It's difficult for me to let people get close to me.
10. I don't want my partner to rely on anyone else but me.
11. I would rather please other people than please myself.
12. When a relationship starts getting intimate, I want to leave.
13. I hold on tightly to my relationships.
14. I am always worried that my partner is going to dump me.
15. I want my partner to need me as much as I need them.
16. I only feel worthy if my partner is satisfied with me.
17. If my partner asked me to stop seeing my friends, I would.
18. I value my ideas and opinions as much as I value my partner's.
19. I don't think I will ever find a partner better than the one I've got, so I will do anything to keep them.

20. When my partner can't help me with something, I feel resentful.

21. I prefer my partner to remain at arm's length.

22. I am happy when my partner depends on me alone.

23. I compromise my values if they are in conflict with my partner's.

24. There is no point getting close to someone because I'll probably get hurt.

25. I would be devastated if my partner left me.

26. When my partner disapproves, I give in.

27. I can't make decisions unless I'm sure of my partner's opinion.

28. I would rather hide my pain than reveal it and risk rejection.

29. I am attracted to people who have serious issues, such as addictions.

30. I am always giving people advice whether they ask for it or not.

31. I find it hard to sleep because I am always worrying about whether my partner loves me.

32. I need to be in full control of my partner's life because they can't function without me.

33. People don't feel comfortable getting close to me in a relationship.

34. I find it difficult to put all my trust in a romantic partner.

35. I am constantly worried that my partner will leave me.

36. I fear that my partner would no longer want to be with me if I told them how I really felt.

37. I feel that I am completely responsible for my partner's happiness.

38. I know what I want without relying on my partner's opinion.

39. I tell my partner what they should and should not do.

40. Before I make a decision, I need a lot of reassurance from others.

41. I am not willing to compromise in a relationship.

42. When I am in a relationship, I make my partner uncomfortable because I am too clingy.

43. I don't feel comfortable if I don't have complete control in the relationship.

44. I get nervous when a romantic partner wants to get too close emotionally.

45. I put the needs of others first before my own needs.

46. I make sure I don't say or do anything that will offend my partner, even if my concerns are valid.

47. I have to change my true character, or my partner won't accept me and leave.

48. I ignore my personal problems and put all my energy into helping my partner.

49. I would leave my partner if they were to mistreat me continuously.

50. I am afraid that I won't be able to function without my partner.

Once you've answered all the questions, add up your score and compare it to the following.

1–50 = Secure attachment style

51–100 = Anxious attachment style

101–150 = Avoidant attachment style

151–250 =Disorganized attachment style

How to Improve Your Attachment Style

If you suffer from relationship anxiety, you are more likely to have a negative attachment style that leads you to act out in ways that make it difficult for you to have a successful partnership. At this moment in time, you have probably resigned yourself to the fact that you are never going to find the man or woman you want to spend the rest of your life with. This couldn't be further from the truth. The problem isn't that relationships are difficult, the problem is that people make relationships difficult. I used to be that woman who could never get it right until I got to the root of the problem. But once I did, dating became a lot easier. Not only because I was aware of my attachment style, and I had started working on it, but I could also discern the attachment style in the potential partners I would meet. I reclaimed a lot of time because I could tell right off the bat that it wasn't going to work out based on their attachment style. As I've learned, you don't need to remain a victim of your childhood, and outside of therapy, there are things you can start doing now to improve your attachment style. Here are some tips to get you started.

Educate Yourself: The first step in changing to a secure attachment style is to identify your attachment style and educate yourself on it. I have provided more than enough information in this book for you to determine your attachment style. Outside of therapy, I found it very helpful to learn about my attachment style. It helped me make sense of a lot of things I had experienced throughout life. If you are serious about enjoying a fulfilling relationship, you will invest in getting to know more about your attachment style.

Start the Healing Process: As you have read, you developed an insecure attachment style because of the way you were raised. Which can result in having many self-esteem and shame issues. Often, the consequence of this is self-neglect, you don't want to deal with your problems, so you focus on everyone else's needs and pay no attention to yours. Self-sabotage, self-criticism, and self-destructive behaviors may have become the norm for you. The healing process will lay the foundation to begin building a secure attachment style. You can start with the following:

- Write down your negative thoughts. They are often attached to a bad decision that you made which may have had disastrous consequences. Now consider these questions: When you made that decision, did you do what you thought was best at the time? If you could go back to that moment, what would you have done differently?

- Forgive yourself for the things you believe you have done wrong. Holding a grudge against yourself is a terrible way to live. It is a form of self-torture; you invest so much time thinking about your shortcomings when the reality is that you can't change the past. Forgiving yourself means refusing to hold the incident against yourself, wash the incident away in the sea of forgetfulness, and don't visit it again.

- Accept that you are not perfect; when you can accept that you are not perfect and that there is no such thing as perfection, it makes life a lot easier. One of the many reasons why people with an anxious attachment style are so hard on themselves is because they are trying to live up to an ideal that doesn't exist. As I did, you will find that you will apply the same standards on your healing journey. Therefore, instead of focusing on perfection, focus on progress. Don't beat yourself up because you are not "fixed" within a couple of weeks. Your healing is a lifelong process; you are not going to arrive at your destination overnight.

Start Working on Your Self-Esteem

There are many deep-rooted reasons why people suffer from low self-esteem. One of them is that they have an idea of who they want to be in their head, but they can't seem to get there. This creates self-hate, self-disgust, and a host of other negative emotions. When I started on my healing journey, I was terribly overweight; my thing was comfort eating. Every night, I would sit in front of the TV and stuff my face with cookies, chips, and soda. I felt great while I was eating them, but reality would sink in when I looked in the mirror, and I hated myself. And I mean with a passion, I couldn't stand the reflection that stared back at me. The depression was so intense, I felt as if I was suffocating. When I made up my mind that I wanted to get better, losing weight was the first thing on my agenda. I set a goal to lose 50 pounds in 12 months by losing one pound a week, and it worked! I changed my eating habits, I started exercising, and I drank more water. As the weight started dropping off, my confidence grew; then, I started moving on to other goals and achieving them. I realized that the only person responsible for my transformation was myself. When it comes to building your self-esteem, I would advise that you start with goal setting; set one small goal, devise a plan, and start working towards it.

Change Your Narrative

We speak to ourselves more than we speak to anyone else; that negative self-chatter in your mind can become so loud that you can't hear anything else. The more you hear these lies about yourself, the more you believe them and start living them out. Changing the way you think is probably one of the most difficult things you will ever do because, for one, the majority of our thoughts are unconscious, and two, you've become so comfortable with hearing the voice of negativity that anything else sounds like an imposter. Think about it like this. Most people know their mother's voice. When she phones and you see her name pop up on the screen, you answer it expecting to hear her voice. But if you hear a voice you don't recognize, the first thing you are going to do is ask where your mother is, and then possibly put down the phone. The same thing will happen when you start speaking kindly to yourself. You won't recognize the voice. It will feel uncomfortable, and you will shut it off. Keep practicing, and it will eventually become the norm.

Now, since the majority of our thoughts are unconscious, and we are so comfortable with our conscious thoughts that we just accept them as the norm, the most effective way of changing your narrative is through daily affirmations. With affirmations, you are making a conscious decision to speak kindly about yourself. Eventually, you will start believing what you are saying, and you will learn to silence your negative inner critic with powerful positive affirmations. Start and end each day reciting these affirmations. I write them on cards and carry them around with me. When I worked in an office, I would say them just before I got out of my car, when I went on my break, and when I got back in my car. I was determined to break the habit of negative thinking. Here are some of my favorite affirmations:

- I am strong, confident, and full of power.
- Everything I need is within me.
- I am full of possibilities and abundance.
- I am moving in the right direction; I am on the right path.
- I believe in my ideas and that I am capable of achieving them.
- I possess the gifts and talents that the world needs.

- I am not my past failures, I can't change my past, but I can change my future.

Working on yourself marks the beginning of your healing journey. I can't tell you the road is going to be easy, but if you and your partner have both made the decision to free yourself from relationship anxiety, the following chapters will provide you with the tools you need to be successful.

Chapter 3: Step 1: How to Overcome Jealousy

"Surrounded by the flames of jealousy, the jealous one winds up, like the scorpion, turning the poisoned sting against himself." ~ Friedrich Nietzsche

Destructive jealousy is a negative trait that has its roots in childhood trauma. Jealousy in itself is a normal healthy emotion, and when it is channeled in the right direction, it can be beneficial. However, it can become a problem when you feel as if you are disadvantaged in some way because you don't have access to the things other people have. For example, you might have experienced the following as a child:

- Your brother or sister received preferential treatment from your parents
- You always got the worst birthday presents
- Your friends' parents were wealthier than yours
- You never had the right toys in school

Children don't understand these emotions. All they know is that it doesn't feel good. If parents fail to teach their kids to channel these emotions in a positive direction, the child will internalize these feelings, withdraw, or act out. These behaviors will resurface in adult relationships, and this is how jealousy becomes destructive.

When Jealousy Becomes Destructive

Author of the book *In the Name of Love* and former professor of philosophy, Aaron Ben-Zeev, states that jealousy in a relationship is rooted in the fear of not being good enough. These insecurities lead a person to believe that their partner will leave them for someone more appealing. During the research phase before writing his book, Ben-Zeev discovered that when a person is dating someone who is emotionally unavailable, they get caught in the trap of wanting more out of the relationship and the fear of losing their partner. As a result, they risk developing what psychologists have termed morbid jealousy.

When jealousy becomes pathological, it causes irrational emotions, and thoughts and behaviors become obsessive. Research suggests that this type of jealousy is more common in older males, and it typically begins around the age of 38.

Joey is a builder; he is married to Hilary, and they have three beautiful children. But Joey has an anxious attachment style, and because of his fear of abandonment, he was terrified that his wife would leave him. So, despite the fact that he barely makes enough to cover the bills, he refuses to allow Hilary to go out and work. She is a qualified teacher, and the children are of school age, so the scenario is ideal for her to go back to teaching. He calls her several times a day to check she hasn't gone anywhere. She's not allowed to wear makeup unless her husband is with her. He even controls who she speaks to on the phone. Even though Hilary describes herself as having a secure attachment, his behavior is giving her severe anxiety. Every month she watches Joey struggle to pay the bills and grow increasingly frustrated with not being able to look after the family the way he would like to. It's a vicious cycle with no end in sight.

Jealousy can become the most destructive emotion housed in the human psyche. According to research, it's the number one cause of spousal killing in the world. This year alone, there have been several crimes of passion. In January 2021, jealous husband Wilfred Jacob stabbed his wife, Linda, to death. He had become convinced that she was having an affair with an ex-partner who had just moved to the county. As her husband's jealous behavior became more threatening, Linda told her husband that she was going to end the marriage. He responded by stabbing her twice in the back with a kitchen knife. Reports suggest that Jacob had no evidence his wife was having an affair. His jealousy stemmed from an idea he had developed in his mind, and someone's life was taken because of it. The following studies might be able to offer some insight into how a person can become so destructive it can lead to murder.

Jealousy Chemicals: Oxytocin is referred to as the trust, love, and cuddle hormone. Studies suggest that the effects of this hormone depend on the context. When it is associated with negative feelings, a release of this hormone can trigger emotional turmoil. A 2009 study conducted by *Biological Psychiatry* examined a group of participants who were induced with oxytocin or a placebo before playing in a competitive game with high stakes. They found that participants who had been defeated but were high on oxytocin felt more resentful and envious than the control placebo group. The results of the study indicate that how chemicals affect us is dependent on how we perceive the social situation we are in.

Several studies have found that when a woman in a relationship with a man has a sexual affair with another man, it triggers jealousy in men, whereas women are more triggered by emotional affairs by their male partners than sexual infidelity. In evolutionary terms, men experience jealousy in this way because they fear wasting their resources on another man's child. On the other hand, when a man has an emotional attachment to another woman, they are at risk of losing their provider. However, Pennsylvania State psychologists Kristen Kelly and Kenneth Levy believe this evolutionary explanation is too simplistic. According to their studies, they have found that there are large numbers of men who become extremely jealous when they find out their partner is having an emotional affair with another man. In other words, it works both ways. The bottom line is that any threat to your relationship will trigger feelings of jealousy.

Jealousy and Commitment: To get a better understanding of this mystery, Kelly and Levy took their study a step further and compared the jealousy types and attachment styles of men and women. They discovered that participants who labeled themselves as having a phobia of intimacy or self-reliance did not feel as strongly about emotional cheating as they did about sexual cheating. The participants who described themselves as wanting intimacy found that they felt stronger about emotional intimacy than sexual intimacy. Kelly and Levy came to the conclusion that when people are intensely self-reliant, it acts as a defense mechanism that protects them against deep-rooted fear. People who are afraid to make an intimate connection with their partner admitted to having intense feelings of jealousy when the relationship contract had been severely violated. However, they did not experience the same feelings when the violation did not have a sexual element to it.

Steps to Overcome Jealousy

Jealousy is a common problem with all insecure attachment styles, but they manifest slightly differently with each one. Jealousy makes people with an anxious attachment style feel terrible about themselves, and they are more likely to engage in surveillance-style behavior. They will do things like go through their partner's phone, emails, and personal letters. Or they will go to extreme lengths of attaching recording devices to their partner's clothes or have a recording device in the home. People with a disorganized attachment style are more likely to express their jealousy through violence. People who hurt their partners tend to have a disorganized attachment style.

You will never allow your partner to have the freedom to live a fulfilling life if you keep restricting them with jealousy, and the same applies to your own life. Jealousy causes stagnation in a relationship, and if it is left unchecked, it can cause some serious problems. Whichever attachment style you have, jealousy can become a thing of the past if you are willing to work at it.

Be Honest: Overcoming jealousy starts with open communication with each other. One of the symptoms of jealousy is shame; even though your behavior screams jealousy, admitting it is different. The shame comes from acknowledging that your jealousy stems from insecurity because the reality is that you don't feel good enough for your partner. That's a difficult pill to swallow. Having an open discussion about your jealousy is the first step to developing a healthy relationship.

What Are the Underlying Causes? Jealousy is definitely a problem, but if you change your perspective, it can also be a solution. Jealousy can become a window of opportunity that you can look through and gain some clarity into the deeper issues that are going on within you and in your relationship. Oftentimes, the emotion of jealousy is triggered by something seemingly insignificant. You will need to think back to the time when you started feeling jealous. What were the circumstances? It may be that your partner actually broke your trust by telling you a white lie or spending more money than they had originally stated. Small lies of this nature might not seem important, but they open the door to negative thinking. At the time, you didn't want to address the lie because of how minor it was. But in your head, you have started thinking, *What else have they lied about?* And thus, the vicious cycle begins.

As mentioned in the honesty section, you may be projecting your insecurities onto your partner. Or, you might feel envious of their success, but that could be because you know your partner is competing with you, and every time they have a win, they rub it in your face. Whatever the reasons, when you look at jealousy as a solution and work backward to find the trigger that set things off for you, you can be confident that jealousy in your relationship will soon become a thing of the past.

Develop Healthy Coping Skills: How do you react when you start feeling jealous? Do you aggressively confront your partner? Start sneaking around and looking through his belongings? Or maybe you isolate yourself and refuse to speak to your partner? Negative coping skills are common in people with an insecure attachment style because you've never been taught how to deal with your emotions in a healthy way. Here are some healthy coping skills that will help you handle your jealousy more productively.

Cognitive Reframing: Cognitive reframing is a technique used by therapists to transform a person's perspective. Let's say your partner has gone out with friends and you are sitting at home thinking the worst. *He's probably hitting on other women, He's probably buying girls drinks, He's probably gone home with* *someone.* In psychology, this type of thinking is referred to as catastrophizing. It means that you're always thinking the worst when a situation takes place. You can reframe your thinking by doing the following:

- **Ask Questions:** When you are so used to thinking a certain way, it's easy to convince yourself that there's no other way of looking at the situation. Cognitive reframing gets you to ask yourself questions that will put you in a different frame of mind. In the case of your partner going out for drinks with his friends, you could ask yourself, *Have I ever heard that he was out buying drinks for other girls?* Assuming the answer is no, you can then ask, *So why would he start now?* At this point, you are no longer thinking the worst but reminding yourself of all the reasons why you can trust him.

- **Validate Your Emotions:** Even though the aim is to overcome jealousy, you don't try to invalidate or deny your feelings either. This will take you right back to square one. Remember, you developed an insecure attachment style because you were forced to bury your emotions. To overcome jealousy or any other negative emotion, you've got to confront them. Validation means that you acknowledge you are experiencing the emotion of jealousy. You can do this by saying to yourself, "I am jealous because my partner is out, and I am afraid that he is flirting with other women. I acknowledge that when I feel jealous, I imagine that the worst is going to happen, but the reality is that I don't know what is going on. For all I know, he could be having a conversation with his friends about football and not paying any attention to the women that are around."

- **Practice Self-Compassion:** Speak to yourself kindly when you start feeling the emotion of jealousy. Develop healthy self-talk by speaking to yourself in the same way you would speak to a friend who is going through something similar. You would want to alleviate their anxious jealous feelings; therefore, you would say something like, "Your boyfriend loves you; he would never do anything to hurt you," or "You've got a very loyal and honest partner; the behavior you are worried about isn't in their character," or "Think about all the amazing things he's done for you. He's invested so much in this relationship, and he's not about to ruin it now." By focusing on the positive aspects of your relationship, you are speaking to yourself in a way that boosts your confidence instead of tearing it down.

Overcome Jealousy Exercise

My therapist gave this exercise to my partner and me, and it totally revolutionized our relationship.

Choose an evening where there are not going to be any distractions. Get together with your partner and create a relaxing atmosphere. You might want to sit down over dinner with a glass of wine and some soft music playing in the background. Whatever you choose to do, just make sure it's free from stress and conducive to productivity. You will both need a notepad and pen to write down the following:

- **Jealousy in Your Relationship:** How exactly is jealousy ruining your relationship? Write about how it makes you feel personally, how it makes you feel about your partner. Write down all the emotions associated with jealousy and your relationship. It could be anger, frustration, depression, hatred. If you feel as if you are on the brink of leaving the relationship, write that down. Don't hold back.

- **Define Your Ideal Relationship:** At present, jealousy is ruining your relationship, which is why you are reading this book. You both want your relationship to improve, but improvement becomes more realistic when you've got a specific target to work towards. While performing this exercise, it's important to remember that there is no such thing as the perfect relationship. You're not aiming for perfection. The aim of this exercise is to determine what it would take to make you happy moving forwards.

- **Develop Your Ideal Relationship:** Now, write down what you think it would take to develop your ideal relationship. You should both write down how you think your partner can help you to overcome your jealousy. What can your partner do to make you feel more secure? What do you think your partner needs to change about themselves to help develop your ideal relationship?

APPLICATION, APPLICATION, APPLICATION! I can't stress this enough. Developing a healthy relationship is going to take work, so it's essential that you put the above advice into practice consistently. A lot of couples give up early because they didn't see immediate results. You won't see immediate results because this is not an overnight fix. There is no magic pill you can swallow or no wand you can wave. If you want your relationship to change, you will need to invest your time, energy, emotions, and everything you've got if you want the positive outcome you are looking for.

In chapter four, we will discuss how you can overcome the fear of abandonment.

Chapter 4: Step 2: How to Overcome the Fear of Abandonment

"The fear of abandonment forced me to comply as a child, but I'm not forced to comply anymore." ~ Christiana Enevoldsen

The fear of abandonment is a type of anxiety that causes people to engage in fear-based behaviors when they think they are at risk of losing someone. Abandonment issues can have a detrimental effect on an individual's life and relationships.

Signs of Fear of Abandonment

How the fear of abandonment manifests in your life will depend on your attachment style. If you have an anxious attachment style, you may be very clingy, needy, and emotionally reactive. When conflict arises, you interpret it as a sign that your partner is going to leave. To avoid being abandoned, you start engaging in fear-based behavior, such as manipulation. Additionally, when your partner is away for long periods of time, you experience separation anxiety.

If you identify as having an avoidant attachment style, you deal with your abandonment issues by not opening up to your partner, being suspicious, withdrawn, and you shut down to avoid conflict.

Those with a disorganized attachment style deal with their fear of abandonment through control. They will do things like control their partner's every move, tell them who they can socialize with, what to wear, and how to spend their money. On a subconscious level, people with a disorganized attachment style feel that the more control they have over their partner, the less likely they are to leave.

In general, there are several signs that you are suffering from the fear of abandonment. Here are some of them:

People-Pleasing: People pleasers don't like conflict and need constant validation. They avoid conflict because they are afraid to upset the person, which will disrupt the relationship in some way. The people-pleaser gains validation by doing things that will elicit praise and gratitude from people. This is how people pleasers act in general, but when they are in a relationship, the person they are most concerned with pleasing is their partner, and they will go to great lengths to ensure the relationship remains intact. For example, you allow them to constantly violate your boundaries because you are afraid to confront them. Or you compromise your values to keep them happy.

Clinginess: Clingy people find it difficult to be alone. When you are away from your partner, you feel depressed and anxious. To alleviate these feelings, you call or text your partner constantly throughout the day. When your partner goes out without inviting you, you have a tendency to show up so you can let everyone know you are in a relationship with them. You are not just emotionally clingy, but you are physically clingy. Anytime you are with your partner, you've got to be attached to their hip at all times.

Confusion: Steve and Amy have been married for three years. Steve has always had a strong bond with his male friends, and once a month, they make arrangements to go out. Sometimes Amy allows Steve to go out, and sometimes she won't. The problem is that she uses manipulation tactics to make him feel guilty for going out. The day before, Amy will fall down the stairs and pretend as if she's hurt her ankle. Or she will pretend to throw up just before Steve is about to leave the house. When Amy is sick or injured, Steve will call his friends and let them know that he won't be able to make it.

Amy knows that what she is doing is wrong and feels bad any time she stops her husband from going out with his friends. However, she doesn't feel secure when he's out, and instead of communicating this to her husband, she uses manipulation tactics.

Unrealistic Expectations: There is absolutely nothing wrong with having expectations in a relationship. In fact, it would be abnormal if you didn't; after all, you can't allow people to disrespect you, so you've got to set standards in your life. However, when you are not happy with yourself, you expect your partner to make you happy, and that's impossible. Your happiness is your responsibility, and as you get deeper into your healing journey, this will become clear to you.

It's important to understand that your partner is unique. He/she has strengths and weaknesses, which means they are not going to be able to fulfill your every need. Your expectations become unrealistic when you place the burden of your happiness on your partner's shoulders.

Emotional Blackmail: Emotional blackmail is a form of manipulation used to control your partner. There are four types of emotional blackmail, and it's important that you know what they are so you are able to recognize when it is happening in your relationship:

1. The Punisher: You let your partner know what you will do to them if they don't comply with your demands.

2. The Self-Punisher: You make your partner feel guilty by punishing yourself. For example, you won't eat for a couple of days.

3. The Sufferer: You make your partner suffer by dragging your feet on issues that are important to them in order to get them to comply with what you want.

4. The Tantalizer: You promise to reward your partner for agreeing to your demands, but once you've got what you want, you don't deliver on the reward.

How to Overcome Your Fear of Abandonment

The key to overcoming the fear of abandonment is recognizing that you are suffering from it. In this section, I provide you with some helpful tips and strategies to help you deal with your fear of abandonment so you can have a fulfilling and healthy relationship.

Inner Child Healing

I found inner child healing extremely powerful when I was in therapy. It completely transformed my life in many ways and accelerated my recovery.

When a child goes through a traumatic event, and it is left unresolved, that pain is stored in their subconscious mind, and their emotional growth gets stuck at that age. As an adult, anything that triggers similar feelings leads to behavior that resembles the emotional maturity of a child. How you dealt with the trauma as a child will determine how you deal with situations that trigger you as an adult. For example, let's say the state you lived in didn't have enough jobs, so to support the family, your mother traveled to another state to work for half the year. You were six years old the first time your mother left, and it had a terrible effect on you.

When a mother leaves a child at such a young age, unless someone teaches them how to process their emotions, the only way their mind knows how to handle the event is to associate their mother leaving with abandonment. As far as they are concerned, their mother left because they must have done something wrong. The father isn't thinking about the child's emotional well-being; he is in survival mode working two jobs to put food on the table. So I dealt with my emotions by isolating myself. I stopped speaking to my father and my siblings. I would eat my dinner and go to bed. I became very introverted.

Fast forward 25 years later, and isolation was my emotional reaction anytime something triggered those feelings. I would shut down and refuse to speak to my partner.

Inner child healing involves going back to that time in your childhood when you felt abandoned and addressing that trauma. You do this by imagining you are a child and pretending you are the parent who abandoned you. You speak to yourself as a child and tell yourself all the things you would have wanted to hear at that time. You comfort your inner child and teach yourself how to deal with those emotions at that time. I found it helpful to write my inner child a letter. You might find it easier to have a conversation with yourself. Additionally, inner child healing is not a one-time event. It took me over a year to heal from my childhood trauma. To this day, if I ever feel myself getting off track, I go back to this method.

Accept That You Are Worthy of Love

The underlying issue for people who are afraid of abandonment is the feeling that they don't deserve love. It is human nature to want love and to feel loved. The fear of abandonment is rooted in trauma, either in childhood or adulthood. Whatever traumatic event took place has led you to believe that the person left you because you were defective in some way. As a result, you magnify your flaws and convince yourself that your partner doesn't really want you.

The first step in accepting that you are worthy of love is accepting that love is about loving imperfection. Perfection doesn't exist, everyone has flaws, and everyone is weak in some areas of life. Since you are in a relationship, your partner chose to be with you despite how you see yourself, and that's because you are worthy of love.

Become Emotionally Independent

Your relationship doesn't define who you are. It is a part of you, but your identity isn't connected to your partner. Despite the fact that you want to improve your relationship, not end it, embrace the idea of being single because you will never be truly happy in a relationship if you are not truly happy without a partner. Your worth is not based on your relationship. Your worth is based on who you are and the unique gifts and talents you bring to the world.

Becoming emotionally independent is going to be difficult because you are so used to being emotionally dependent. It will involve you taking ownership of your feelings and accepting that no one can make you feel anything you don't allow. You choose how you react to hurt, disappointment, and frustration in your relationship. Fear manifests in the form of jealousy, people-pleasing, and a host of other destructive behaviors. When fear starts to surface, confront those feelings, evaluate them, and ask yourself whether they are rational or not. If they are, address them with your partner using the conflict resolution strategies in Chapter 8. If not, allow yourself to experience the emotion and then let it go.

Additionally, emotional independence means that you no longer look to your partner to make you feel secure. They don't have the power to take your fear away; that's your responsibility.

Abandonment Journal

One way to get to the bottom of your thoughts, emotions, and feelings about your abandonment is through journaling. Your mind is able to process your emotions and fears when you put them down on paper. Once written out, they are no longer distant thoughts that are hard to reach. You can look at them, experience them, and deal with them. Here are some questions to ask yourself while journaling:

- How many times have you felt abandoned in your life? What happened, and how did it make you feel?

- Did you feel that you were abandoned because you had done something wrong?
- What did you tell yourself about the abandonment?
- How has your fear of abandonment affected past relationships?
- How is your fear of abandonment affecting your current relationship?
- What negative behaviors do you think result from your abandonment issues?
- What negative behaviors are you not conscious of (the ones your partner tells you about)?
- What action can you take today to change fear-based negative behaviors?

Accept That You May Always be Fearful

Fear is a natural human emotion, and experiencing it is not the problem. The problem is when you allow the fear to dictate your behavior. Once you understand the root cause of your fear and the unhealthy thought patterns that come along with it, you can work towards managing them. For example, you might spend your time worrying that your partner is attracted to a certain type of man, and since you don't have the six-pack, tanned skin, and dark hair, she is going to leave you as soon as she finds what she wants. You handle these emotions by controlling your partner. You tell her what to wear, refuse to let her go out with her friends, refuse to let her look at magazines, etc.

All of these behaviors originate from your thoughts. So, instead of allowing your thoughts to take over your mind to the point where you act on those thoughts, put a stop to them as soon as you recognize them. You can achieve this through positive self-talk. You can say something like:

- "Even though she has a preference for a certain look, she has chosen to be with me."
- "I can't control who she looks at when she's not with me, so what's the point of trying to control her when she's with me?"
- "She loves me for who I am, not because of what I look like."

Relationship insecurity is another crippling form of anxiety in a relationship. Living in fear that the worse might happen is no fun at all. In the next chapter, we will discuss how you can overcome this.

Chapter 5: Step 3: How to Overcome Relationship Insecurity

"Only the insecure strive for security." ~ Wayne Dyer

She doesn't get excited when she sees me these days. Why have things changed? Weren't we more affectionate at the beginning of our relationship? Why doesn't she find me attractive anymore? Rhetorical questioning is the first phase of relationship insecurity. It also involves questions like, *She's stopped answering the phone straight away. Why doesn't she call me as often when I'm away? Why doesn't she laugh at my jokes anymore? Does she have her eye on someone else?*

Phase two involves blaming yourself for the supposed breakdown of the relationship with thoughts such as *It's because I'm not as ripped as I used to be. I work too much. I'm not as exciting as I used to be. I will never be able to make her happy. She would probably be better off without me.*

As I am sure you are aware, insecurity can be terribly toxic to your relationship, and it's unhealthy for both of you regardless of the role being played. It does not come as a surprise that research suggests people with low self-esteem are more insecure in their relationships. Low self-esteem can prevent a person from enjoying everything that comes with a loving connection with someone. They have a deep need for their partner to prove their love for them because they don't love who they are. But when they constantly doubt everything their significant other says or does, no matter how many reassurances they receive, those words fall on deaf ears. Furthermore, it is the manifestation of your insecurities that will ultimately push your partner away.

When it comes to relationship insecurity, the struggle is an internal one. As has been mentioned several times, your attachment style will determine the quality of your relationships. And one of the expressions of an insecure attachment style is relationship insecurity.

As much as your partner wants to help you overcome your issues, you are the one responsible for your healing. Here are some tips to get you started.

Drop the Baggage

Baggage weighs you down, and a lot of people go into a relationship carrying excess baggage from previous relationships or from life events that have scarred them. According to relationship expert Nicole Martinez, people carry baggage into a relationship when they don't learn from past mistakes. Instead of allowing the experience to teach you what not to do and what not to tolerate in your new relationship, you allow those hurts to keep you stagnant.

Baggage has a lot of negative consequences, and one of them is that you find it difficult to trust your new partner, even though they don't have any of the characteristics of your ex.

Shortly after I had divorced my first husband, I moved to Chicago in search of a new life. I met a guy (we will call him Alfred) on an online dating website. We hit it off instantly and got serious really quickly. I really shouldn't have been dating because I was nowhere near healed from my first relationship, but I was desperately lonely and looking for stability. There were loads of red flags from the beginning, but he was so charming, I ignored them. After a few months, he got really nasty. He would kick me out onto the streets without my coat in the middle of the night (and I'm talking about wintertime Chicago here)! He did loads of awful things to me, and cheating was one of them, but I stayed. I left after he gave me a black eye during a fight.

It took a couple of years before I started dating again, but every time I got into a new relationship, the pain and anxiety would revisit me. I would spend hours agonizing over whether he would be just like Alfred. If a new partner's behavior was in the least bit similar to my ex's, my heart would start beating faster than normal, and I would pick a fight with my partner because I was indirectly trying to push him away. Emotional baggage is the invisible weight we carry due to unresolved traumas or issues from previous relationships. According to clinical psychologist John Duffy, unless we confront these issues and resolve them, we will keep carrying emotional baggage into our new relationships. It was only through therapy that I was able to drop my baggage and move on to greener pastures. Here are the strategies I found useful:

- **Comparison Test:** To start the process of dropping the baggage, get a pen and a notepad and write down everything that went wrong in your last relationship. On another sheet of paper, write down everything that you feel is going wrong in your current relationship. Are there any similarities? If you answer yes, determine whether these similarities are justifiable. With relationship insecurity, you often look for problems that aren't there. For example, if you broke up with your ex-partner because he cheated, and the way he met with his mistress was by claiming he was going to the store every other day, now in your new relationship, any time your partner goes grocery shopping, you accuse him of cheating. This is not a justifiable similarity; you will find that as you write these things down, you will either come to the conclusion that you have got evidence to substantiate your claims, or it's because your emotional baggage is causing you to act this way.

- **Purge:** What have you got in your home that reminds you of your previous relationship? Are there any gifts you've kept? One of the reasons I got trapped in the relationship with Alfred was because he was so generous. When I moved into my new apartment, he bought me a really nice sofa, and I never got rid of it. But my psychiatrist convinced me to throw it out; subconsciously, the sofa reminded me of Alfred, so he was basically an invisible presence in all my relationships because the sofa was symbolic of him. I had got rid of everything else but that sofa, and once I did, I noticed a definite energy shift in my home, and I felt a lot more peaceful mentally. So, whatever you have from your previous relationship, get rid of it.

- **Talk to Your Partner:** It is not uncommon for people to conceal abuse or any other problems from previous relationships because they are afraid of being judged. Letting your significant other know what you went through will do wonders for your relationship. The person on the receiving end of your insecurity can get very frustrated because they don't know where it's coming from. When you don't understand something, you either shut it out or judge incorrectly. But eventually, you will get fed up with being accused of something you haven't done and leave the relationship. Have an open discussion with your partner about what you went through in your past and give them the opportunity to be more compassionate with you. And it might not even be about abuse. It could just be general behaviors that you find difficult to deal with, such as lateness. Let's say your previous partner was late for everything because that was his way of letting you know that he wasn't truly committed to the relationship. As a result, you now fly off the handle any time your partner is late, even if it's only rarely. By telling your partner what you feel his lateness represents because of what you went through in the past, they will make more of an effort to change.

Balance Your Polarity

Most people have never heard of the word polarity, so let me explain. Polarity is the pull or attraction we feel towards a person whose energy is opposite to ours. In a romantic relationship, polarity is determined by masculine and feminine energy. When two people have similar polarities, they are not as attracted to one another. When there is a clear polarity between partners, their sexual attraction thrives. Okay, so what has this got to do with relationship insecurity? If your polarity is out of balance, you are not going to have a strong sexual desire for each other; you will sense it, and your insecurity will intensify. The question now becomes, how do we balance our polarity? You were probably in balance at one time, which is why you were attracted to each other, so now you've got to get back in balance. Let's start with tips for masculine energy.

Lift Weights: Lifting weights boosts the masculine mindset. Not only does challenging your body promote mental strength, but it also triggers the release of high levels of testosterone, which helps increase self-confidence, motivation, and sex drive. A study conducted by UCLA found that four weeks of weightlifting caused a 40% increase in resting testosterone, and it reduced cortisol by 24%. Burning fat and building muscle makes men look and feel better, which makes them more attractive to women.

Play Sports: The healthy practice of aggression enables men to tap into their masculine energy, and one way to do this is through playing sports. Martial arts also help men embrace their inner masculinity. It brings out their animalistic raw side and makes them feel as if they can take on the world.

Have Man Time: Men feed off each other's energy. Evolutionary research argues that men only reveal who they truly are when they're with other men. Spending time with men allows them to speak openly about how they feel and take part in activities they are passionate about.

Femininity is expressed through a woman's inborn desire towards compassion, caring, and connection. Here are three ways a woman can awaken her feminine energy:

Create a Space with Love: Create a loving area in your home that's just for you. Feminine energy responds well to this type of environment. Spend time in this area daily and get in touch with your divine power through things like meditation, journaling, listening to soft music, and lighting candles. During this time, set your intentions for how you desire your life to be. When you prioritize self-care, you deepen the connection you have with yourself.

Move Your Body: Feminine energy is fluid; it's not stagnant. A stagnant body causes trapped emotions. The inability to express yourself hinders feminine energy. Surrender to movement through dancing, yoga, walking, or stretching.

Connect with Your Feelings: Allowing, feeling, and expressing your feelings activates feminine energy. Allow yourself to be vulnerable and connect with your feelings without judgment. Listen to what your feelings are saying and express yourself accordingly. In this way, your decision-making is going to be in alignment with your higher self.

Stop Overanalyzing Everything

You're washing the dishes, and your partner walks into the kitchen to grab a drink. She doesn't say a word to you, just walks in, gets what she came for, and walks out. Looking at this situation objectively, it's pretty normal. There's absolutely nothing wrong with it. She's thirsty. She got a drink and went back to what she was doing. No big deal. But to you, it's not normal, and your immediate assumption is that she's angry with you and your thoughts start to wonder. *Did I say something wrong at dinner? Maybe I didn't put the toilet seat down? Did I make the bed properly this morning?* This is what experts refer to as overanalyzing. Psychiatrist Maureen

Sayres states, "Overanalyzing is like a constant record player in the mind of negative self-examination."

There is nothing wrong with examining your relationship. Worry and anxiety are natural emotions, and it's normal to have them from time to time. However, it becomes a problem when it's over nothing and constant. Not only is it a drain on your mental energy, but it also damages the relationship. Overanalyzing doesn't stop with thoughts. With the above example, once her partner finished washing the dishes, he would have gone and started an unnecessary argument with his girlfriend. Your bad habit of overanalyzing everything isn't going to stop overnight, but you've got to start somewhere, so here are a few tips:

Understand the Root Cause: I am no stranger to overanalyzing my relationships. I used to think it was my way of finding the solution to a problem I imagined we were having. I would zone in on something my partner had said or done, but my thoughts would just go around in circles, and I never came to a conclusion. My thoughts just made my relationship problems appear more overwhelming and scarier, and they became a vicious cycle of fear and doubt. I later learned that overthinking was about fear, doubt, and panic.

Focus on Your Feelings: Your gut is going to communicate with you better than your thoughts. If the root cause of overanalyzing is doubt, fear, and panic, your feelings will let you know what you are really concerned about. In other words, there is a deeper problem in your relationship, and your feelings will let you know what that is.

What Are Your Fears?: There is something in your relationship that you are worried about, or your feelings wouldn't be telling you something was wrong. Some of the fears that had me overthinking were:

- Fear of marrying someone like my dad
- Fear that my partner didn't really love me
- Fear of getting trapped in an unhappy relationship

At this point, you can start strategizing. What are you going to do to make sure these fears don't become your reality? My parents were always arguing, and they were verbally abusive to each other. I could avoid having this problem in my relationship by learning how to communicate with my partner in the right way.

When you listen to your feelings, you will find out what your fears are, and then you can work out a plan of action to offset them.

Think about the Context: How ironic, the remedy to stop overthinking is to think! The idea is to draw a conclusion about why you're thinking this way about the situation. Using the example of doing the dishes and your partner walking in without saying anything to you, think about it like this. If you've been in the house for a couple of hours and she hasn't displayed any signs of being annoyed or frustrated with you, it would make no sense to assume she's angry because you didn't make the bed in the morning.

Change the Record: Once you've come to your senses, and drawn the conclusion that you are being irrational, now you can stop thinking about it. Stop thinking about all the reasons she might be angry with you and how you are going to confront the situation once you've washed the dishes. Focus your mind on something positive, like the great weekend you are about to have or the pretty flowers you plan on buying her on your way back from work.

Reverse Black and White Thinking

Black and white thinking is the inability to look at the gray area in a situation. It's an extreme way of thinking that concludes something like, *My girlfriend is either an angel or a demon.* According to the American

Psychological Association, black and white thinking is considered to be a cognitive distortion due to the fact that it hinders us from seeing the world as it really is: nuanced, complex, and with plenty more shades than just black and white. It is very difficult to maintain a healthy lifestyle when you think in such extremes, and it will ultimately destroy your relationship. You may find it helpful to try the following techniques to stop black and white thinking.

List Options: What are the two options you have given yourself? Write them down on a piece of paper, one at the top of the page, the other at the bottom of the page. Now fill in the gap with different options. You may not be able to come up with more than one, but that's okay. At least you don't have zero.

Reality Reminders: When black and white thinking has got you stuck, say out loud, or write down a factual statement such as, "There are many different ways I can resolve this problem. If I spend more time thinking about this, I will make a better decision."

Get a Second Opinion: If the issue you are having is with your partner, speaking to them about it at this stage probably isn't a good idea, so call a friend or a family member to get a second opinion. Someone from the outside looking in is going to evaluate your situation objectively and provide you with different options.

The next step in overcoming relationship anxiety is to repair the trust that may have been broken or develop trust that was never there. In Chapter 6, you will learn exactly how to do this.

Chapter 6: Step 4: How to Rebuild Trust in Your Relationship

"He who does not trust enough will not be trusted." ~ Lao Tzu

When you trust your partner, you feel safe and secure. But when you've got anxiety about your relationship, you are not going to feel secure. Additionally, no one is perfect, so there may be things you or your partner have done to erode trust, such as broken promises and lies, even if they were just white ones. A part of finding freedom in your relationship involves building trust. Also, trust is difficult for people with an insecure attachment style.

If you have an anxious attachment style, it is possible that the slightest little issue will have you thinking your partner is having an affair. You monitor their every last move, and you demand to be with them all the time. Behavior of this nature is rooted in the belief that the people you love always leave and that you don't really deserve to be happy.

Those with an avoidant attachment style don't trust people, so they refuse to open up emotionally for fear of getting hurt. You really want to trust your partner, but you have been subconsciously blocked from doing so.

People with a disorganized attachment style carry a burden of betrayal and have built walls around themselves to ensure they are never betrayed again. They view everything as a rejection and will abandon a relationship if they perceive a problem. There won't be a discussion about it; they will just leave and block you on all platforms. People with a disorganized attachment style have very complex trust issues because they were typically raised in abusive households, and they desperately want to avoid feeling that level of betrayal by the person they love and who is supposed to love them.

Whether the trust in your relationship has been broken or you are learning how to trust your partner, regardless of your attachment style, you can develop a healthy trusting union with your significant other by applying the following methods:

Allow Yourself to be Vulnerable: Two employees who have worked in an office together for five years, but have never collaborated on a major project, might engage with each other on a surface level and have conversations about the weather. But their connection won't go any further than that. Whereas two co-workers may have only worked together for six months but the intensity of the project they are working on means they've got to rely on each other for some pretty important stuff. They've got to call each other after hours, make sure deadlines are met, and sometimes argue when things are not working out as planned. Despite the short amount of time they've been working together, these two employees will have developed a solid bond because they've had to be vulnerable with each other and rely on each other during crucial times, or the project would fall through. The co-workers with a superficial relationship have never had the opportunity to develop a strong bond.

In your relationship, you build trust through vulnerability. People with an insecure attachment style find vulnerability difficult because whether they realize it or not, they are subconsciously trying to avoid developing trust. However, emotional vulnerability is extremely important in a relationship. You must be willing to open up to your partner despite the risk of getting hurt. You can start with small things like talking about things that scare you, showing your partner parts of your body you are insecure about, or discussing an embarrassing situation from your past. You will never know if you trust your partner because trust is only built by giving your partner the chance to let you down, but they don't. Do this gradually, and as you feel more comfortable becoming more vulnerable, do so.

Don't Go Back on Your Word: This principle starts with yourself. One of the reasons why people are so insecure is they don't trust themselves. If you are always making promises to yourself and breaking them, you will see yourself as unreliable. Think about it like this: When a friend tells you they are going to meet you at the station at 5 p.m., but for three days in a row they don't turn up, you are going to draw the conclusion that they are unreliable, and you will be justified in doing so. When you keep telling yourself you are going to wake up at 5 a.m. and go to the gym, but you never do, you are not going to trust anything you say. If you can't trust yourself, how can you expect your partner to trust you? You can compare expecting your partner to trust you when you don't trust yourself to telling your loved one to sit on a broken chair knowing full well it's broken and they are going to end up on the floor!

You can practice following through on your word by giving yourself small tasks and completing them. The idea is not to overwhelm yourself. You are more likely to do ten sit-ups a day than 100, so start small and work your way up.

Be Respectful: Everyone has their own definition of respect, but for argument's sake, let's take a look at how the dictionary defines it. According to the English dictionary, it means: "Due regard for the feelings, wishes or rights of others." One thing I do know about respect is that it's a two-way street. You've got to give respect to earn it and vice versa. Nevertheless, I'm sure neither you nor your partner is a mind reader, which is why communication is essential to giving each other the respect you both deserve.

Anthea and David are in their late twenties. They have been together for three years and have started talking about marriage. Despite the fact that they've got a lot of issues, they want to make their relationship work. But they have one major problem that is hindering them from saying "I do," which is why they go and see a relationship counselor. That problem is disrespect.

When Anthea is asked why she feels David disrespects her, she says:

"If we are having a conversation about something we disagree with, he will tell me that my opinion is 'nonsense.' He makes me feel that my opinion is worthless because it's different from his. Because of how he makes me feel, I would rather not have discussions about things that are important to me."

David admits that he mocks Anthea's opinions and makes her feel bad, but he didn't feel comfortable admitting this and gave the following response:

"I didn't know I was hurting her feelings by expressing my opinions. I thought having healthy debates was good for relationships."

The counselor went on to ask David:

"But now that Anthea has told you how she feels, can you see that you are judging her by labeling her opinion as nonsense? Can you also see that your behavior is causing her to become withdrawn and introverted? Can you understand why Anthea would feel disrespected?" David agreed that he could see how he was making his partner feel.

Because David can now see things from Anthea's point of view, she feels comfortable expressing herself further and states:

"He can become a bit aggressive when he wants affection and I'm not in the mood. When I say no, he refuses to speak to me."

The counselor asks David: "Can you see how it's disrespectful to get aggressive with your partner when she doesn't feel like being intimate with you? Can you see that you are asking her to do something she isn't comfortable with?"

David responded: "I had never looked at it like that because I assumed since we were in a committed relationship, it was my right to have an intimate connection with her. But now I understand why she needs to be in agreement with me first."

The counselor then asked David to talk about how he feels Anthea is disrespectful towards him in the relationship.

David said, "My problem is that she does small things to disrespect me, and after a while, I lose my temper. You always tell me what I think or feel without asking. Also, you can't seem to keep our personal business in the home. When anything goes wrong, you get on the phone and start telling our friends and your family. I find that to be extremely disrespectful."

Anthea agreed with everything David said and took full responsibility for making him feel disrespected. The counselor advised that they don't have a major issue at the moment, but if things continue like this, eventually, they will become unbearable, and the relationship will break down.

The problem with David and Anthea is that there was no agreement in place about respect, and they didn't understand each other's expectations. Having a mutual understanding is a part of the foundation for all relationships. As you can see from the above example, couples are going to disagree, and there is nothing wrong with this, especially when the concept of acceptance is embraced. You and your partner will both have a different way of thinking and a different set of values because you are individuals. However, you have no right to judge your partner if you don't agree with their opinion. You must treat each other with honor, listen to each other, and show that you respect and value each other's opinions.

Life is unpredictable. Sometimes it can catch us off guard, and without being intentionally cruel or without meaning to disrespect or harm anyone, we can push our opinions onto people and violate their boundaries. Once the violation has taken place, trust is broken. Now we want to protect ourselves, and we do this by withdrawing. Isolation leads to bitterness, and at this point, it becomes difficult to resolve the problems you are having in your relationship.

It's really important that you talk to each other about how you want to be respected. You should also discuss how other people have violated your boundaries in the past so that your partner gets a clear understanding of what respect means to you. As a couple, you should both make a dedicated commitment to making certain that mutual respect is grounded in your relationship. You can achieve this by continuously clarifying your needs, boundaries, and desires because your partner might forget. Remembering what we need is never an issue, but remembering what other people need can become problematic if we are not reminded. Having regular open discussions will help refresh your and your significant others' memories.

If you feel that respect is lacking in your relationship, the following exercise will help you establish it.

- **Make a list of the reasons why you are attracted to each other. Don't include looks.**

  There is a reason why you are still together; as with most couples, the initial attraction was physical, and as you got to know each other and discover each other's unique personalities and character traits, your feelings for each other intensified. Go back to those qualities, write them down, and then read them back to each other. After a while, you will start improvising and praising and adoring each other because feelings that were buried will start coming to the surface.

- **Room for Improvement:** Personal accountability is difficult; in general, we don't like looking within and focusing on our weaknesses. People tend to get offended when character traits that need improving are pointed out. However, despite the fact that it's a difficult pill to swallow, it's necessary. If your relationship is going to improve, that improvement must first start with you. Since everything you do affects your partner, they will be more aware of your faults than you. Therefore, you should both write down character traits for each other that you think need improving. Don't hold back here, be open and honest because a strong relationship is all about supporting each other to become the best versions of yourself.

- **What Does Respect Mean?:** As mentioned, everyone has their own definition of respect. Communicating this to your partner is important because, as you have learned from the above example, both partners were disrespecting each other, but none of them were aware of it. Write down your definitions of respect and share them with one another. Make sure you are both clear about what respect means to your partner.

Forgive Your Partner: Forgiveness is a touchy subject when it comes to people with an insecure attachment style. People with an anxious attachment style get emotionally hijacked and find emotional regulation difficult. But when they do get in touch with their emotions, they will spend a lot of time visiting the past. In other words, if your partner has an anxious attachment style, they are not going to keep reminding you of what you've done to them because of the strong emotions they have attached to the event. Psychologists refer to this as revolving anger. Before they reach a state of forgiveness, the anxiously attached will need to keep processing the negative emotion. Once the bad feelings surrounding the transgression have been released, they will forgive. So when apologizing to your partner, first, you can't do so half-heartedly, and second, they will need time to process the apology once it's been delivered.

With an avoidant attachment style, you will need to get a clear understanding of why you are apologizing. The desire to be forgiven so your partner is no longer angry with you isn't enough. If the person with an avoidant attachment style is being apologized to, they are likely to get very defensive, and the confrontation could escalate as feelings of anger are expressed. This is not the time to walk away. You will need to remain physically and emotionally present, do not respond with aggression, and listen actively.

All people with an insecure attachment style feel uncomfortable when they are vulnerable. But the person with the disorganized attachment style feels even more uncomfortable with it because they do not like acknowledging their wrongdoing or weakness; additionally, interpersonal conflict is something they shy away from. They tend to blame the victim when something goes wrong instead of taking responsibility for their actions.

Moving forward requires complete forgiveness, or you will remain stuck in the past. One of my relationships was ruined because I didn't know how to forgive. My partner had done something I wasn't happy with. He gave his phone number to a girl on a drunken night out with his friends. I found out because when she phoned, he was in the shower and I answered it. She had no idea he was in a relationship and was very apologetic about the whole situation. I made sure to ask her if they had gotten physical on the night; she said no, and I believed her, as she had no reason to lie to me. When my partner came out of the shower, he received my full wrath. The argument went on for weeks. We slept in separate rooms, we spent days not talking—it was a mess. We finally decided to have a discussion about it. He managed to convince me it was because he was drunk, and since he didn't get physical with the woman, it didn't count as cheating. Obviously, I was insecure and naive and decided to forgive him and stay in the relationship. However, I had no idea what forgiveness meant, and any time we got into an argument, I brought it up. He eventually got tired of my behavior and left, but it was a lesson learned. So when it comes to forgiveness, the first step is actually knowing what it means.

What is Forgiveness? Most people have no idea what forgiveness really means, the assumption is that the offender makes a sincere apology, it's accepted, and that's the end of the matter. But true forgiveness is much more than this. It involves the perpetrator acknowledging the wrong they have done and apologizing, but the person who has been offended is responsible for putting forgiveness into action.

Forgiveness is about letting go of the desire for revenge. When the person you love hurts you, it's difficult. You want them to feel the same pain you've felt. There are some relationships that operate on this tit-for-tat principle. One person makes a mistake, the other will do the same until they either break up or get help. I once heard a saying that, "Unforgiveness is like drinking poison and expecting the other person to die." In other words, the only person you are hurting when you refuse to forgive is yourself. You become an angry and bitter person who lives in the past. Meanwhile, the person who has caused the offense has moved on from what they've done. Unfortunately, there is no button we can press to erase a bad memory. You are not going to forget what your partner has done, but how you choose to use those thoughts is up to you. When someone hasn't forgiven a person for what they've done, they do things like get angry because they are thinking about what happened, or they keep reminding their partner about what they did.

Forgiveness is a process, and it starts by getting a clear understanding of the events that took place. What made your partner act in the way they did? And why were you offended? Once your partner has acknowledged their wrongdoing and articulated this to you, your next step is to make the decision to forgive them. But only make this decision once you have a full understanding of the events that took place because an important aspect of forgiveness is throwing the transgression into the sea of forgetfulness and refusing to revisit it again. This means you are forbidden from bringing it up with your partner, and perhaps the most difficult aspect of forgiveness is refusing to reminisce over the event and revisit old emotions. Forgiveness takes work, but if you are willing and committed, it's more than possible.

Give Each Other Time: Rebuilding and developing trust takes time. It's not going to happen overnight, and this is especially true if you or your partner have done something to damage the trust in your relationship. You are both going to need to vent the hurt, anger, and frustrations that you are currently experiencing and that you've held in over time. You will need to ask each other questions, have deep discussions, and peel back old wounds. This phase will take time, and you should both be compassionate and understanding to each other. Refrain from making comments such as, "Why are you still hung up over this?" People deal with things at their own pace, and you have no right to put a time frame on your partner's healing. You also need to be sympathetic to the fact that they have had a difficult life and they have just started their self-development journey. You are both going to have your challenges, there are areas where you will struggle and need grace, and there are areas where your partner will struggle and need grace. Compromise and compassion are two very important elements when it comes to building trust.

Be Sensitive to Their Needs: In order to make your partner feel safe and secure in the relationship, sensitivity to each other's needs is essential. Your partner might ask for full access to your phone and emails. They may require that you don't stay out late on Friday nights or that you don't go out of the room to have private conversations with friends. In some cases, you might think that your partner's requests are extreme, but if you want to make the relationship work and you want your partner to trust you, this is what you will need to do. You should also bear in mind that as you and your partner start trusting each other more, a lot of the extreme requests will not be required. After a while, you will find that your partner no longer needs full access to your phone, emails, letters, etc.

Take Responsibility for Your Actions: Playing the blame game is not how you build trust. Pointing fingers at each other and accusing your partner of doing things that led you to do what you did will not benefit you. First and foremost, most people are not going to take responsibility for something they know they haven't done. Therefore, playing the blame game leads to a vicious cycle that you will never escape. The best way to handle any issues that you are having is to look within. Take personal accountability for where you are in life. How can you make better decisions? What things can you change to make sure this doesn't happen again? Personal accountability will free you from the victim mentality.

The Three As: Attention, appreciation, and affection will take you a long way. Romance doesn't require that you spend a lot of money; the small loving gestures you make all mean something. One of the greatest complaints from women is that their partners only show affection when they want sex. I am not making a generalization here, I am simply stating what I have seen, experienced, and heard. If you are a man reading this, the worst thing you can do is only show your partner affection when you want sex. Women don't respond to this, and they will quickly shut down if you are going to take this approach. Men also need attention, appreciation, and affection, but they need it in a different way. Men show their love by doing things for you: fixing the sink, going to the store in the middle of the night, etc., are all ways in which men show you that they care. In many cases, women have a bad habit of writing these acts of kindness off as "men's work." In other words, that's just what men do; it's nothing special. But it is, and you should show your partner you appreciate him for doing these things. Additionally, women need to feel appreciated when they do things like cook dinner, wash the dishes, and do laundry. Again, these things are written off as women's work, and men take them for granted. In the 1950s, this might have been acceptable, but in today's world, things are different, and a lot of women will refuse to do these things if they think they are being taken advantage of.

Instead of spending hours in front of the TV, on the phone, or playing video games, give your partner some undivided attention and affection. Give them a back massage, brush their hair, run them a bath. Do things that are going to make your partner want to spend time with you.

In any relationship, communication is key, but a lot of couples find this difficult because they don't speak the same language. "Both me and my partner speak English," I hear you saying. I am not talking about your vernacular; I am referring to your love language. Keep reading to find out exactly what I mean...

Chapter 7: Step 5: Get to Know Your Love Language

"Listen with ears of tolerance! See through the eyes of compassion! Speak with the language of love." ~ Rumi

When was the last time you sat down with a person who you knew didn't speak English and attempted to have a full-blown conversation with them? Never, right? Why waste your time unless you have an interpreter? There's no point because you won't understand them, and they won't understand you. Well, how would you feel if I were to tell you that you are probably living this scenario out with your partner every day? Even though you both speak English, the way you express your love for each other might be different, and as a result, you feel disconnected from your significant other.

I felt this way for a long time, no matter what relationship I was in, and I could never figure out what the problem was. You see, my primary love language is words of affirmation, and so any time I found a partner, I would spend my days sending soppy text messages, and they were never reciprocated. They either wouldn't reply, or they would send a thumbs up or reply with "I'll see you later," and I would get offended.

When I started therapy, I was given a book called *The Five Love Languages: The Secret to Love That Lasts* by marriage counselor Dr. Gary Chapman, and I discovered a fundamental truth about my relationship practices, which was that I had zero understanding of love languages. Additionally, it is equally as important that I understood my partner's love language. Once you find out your partner's love language, it's literally like learning a second language. You know how to express love in your language, but you don't know how to express love in your significant other's language, and it's going to take some work.

Love languages give you a better idea of what's most important to your partner and what can really hurt them. For example, my second love language is quality time (more on this later), when my partner would talk on the phone or send messages when we were on a date. Or when he would look around the room when we were talking, I felt unappreciated because he wasn't giving me his undivided attention.

Chapman states that after 30 years of marriage counseling, he had come to the conclusion that there are five emotional love languages, and this is how people communicate and understand emotional love. He argues that it is rare for a couple to have the same love language. As should be expected, we speak our primary love language and expect our partner to understand what we are expressing. When they don't, we get confused and wonder if our partner really loves us. Chapman believes that understanding each other's love language can improve relationship satisfaction and help create an environment where conflict resolution is easier. Couples also find that they bring out the best in each other when they are speaking the same language. As mentioned, there are five primary love languages, and they are as follows:

Words of Affirmation

Do you or your partner get excited about and place a high amount of significance on the spoken and written word? Do you feel all warm inside when your partner demonstrates sweet expressions of encouragement, gratitude, compliments, and appreciation? If you have answered yes to any of these questions, there's a high chance that your main love language is words of affirmation.

Words of affirmation are provided in either spoken or written form, and they support, confirm, empathize with, or uplift another person in a positive way. According to family and marriage therapist Michele DeMarco, people gravitate towards words of affirmation as a love language because they believe that words are powerful, and they give feelings a voice. Positive reinforcement through praise or compliments that highlight who they are as a person or the things they have done or are doing gives them a great sense of fulfillment. Underneath every word is an ocean of significance and meaning, working to either strengthen or weaken the bond they have with their partner.

Appreciation is the driving force behind words of affirmation. It recognizes substance over appearance and quality over quantity. It promotes compassion and empathy and causes intimacy to thrive. Words of affirmation keep the person who speaks this love language calm and grounded. It's all about inclination. What is your natural way of being? How do you express how you feel?

Words of Affirmation When You Are in a Relationship

Not everyone is good with words, but if you want to put relationship anxiety behind you and develop a strong bond with your partner, it's essential that you learn their love language. I have a friend from Wisconsin who married a Ghanaian woman (Ghana is in West Africa). Her English was good, but there were some things she expressed better in her native language, and he couldn't understand what she was saying. So guess what? My friend spent a year learning her language so that he could communicate with her better! That's the level of commitment you should aspire to when it comes to your love language. Here are a few things you should consider when using words of affirmation.

Consistency: This is not a one-time event; you've got to be consistent with it. It might feel uncomfortable at first because you are not used to it, but as the saying goes, practice makes perfect. Additionally, once you express yourself through words once, your partner will expect it again and feel disappointed when they feel that you are giving them the silent treatment. Also, be sincere with what you are saying, don't say things for the sake of it. Make sure whatever you say comes from the heart and is expressed with passion. In doing so, you will recharge your partner's appetite for affirmation. They will overflow with gratitude, and because they feel supported, it will change their perspective about the relationship for the better.

Write it Down: Not everyone has got the oratory skills of Winston Churchhill, or you might be a better writer than speaker. Some people find it easier to express themselves on paper because it gives them more time to think about what they want to say. What you don't want to do is get stuck for words and repeat something you heard on a film or in a song. I can guarantee you your partner will not appreciate it one bit, especially if they've heard the line before! Take your time to craft something beautiful in a nice card. It will melt your significant other's heart.

Think Before You Speak: We have all heard the saying, "Think before you speak." Well, this couldn't be more important to someone whose primary love language is words of affirmation. Sometimes, the things you say can have the wrong impact, and not because you intended for it to be that way. For example, you might say something like, "You look beautiful in that dress, but the other one makes you look slimmer." Your girlfriend might take this the wrong way, especially if she's sensitive about her weight. That one comment will undo all your previous efforts because the conversation will end up going something like:

"So you're telling me I'm fat?"

"No, babe. I just mean the other dress is more flattering."

"Well, why? Can you see my rolls?"

"Yes, around the back, I think the dress is a bit too tight."

"So I'm fat?

Can you see how quickly that supposed compliment turned sour? You can avoid this by not saying ANYTHING negative at all.

Be Yourself: Your partner knows you inside out and back to front. If you are saying things that don't match your personality, you will defeat the purpose of using words of affirmation because your significant other will feel as if you are not being genuine. Before you say anything, make sure it's something you would say, or go back to the drawing board.

What Does Your Partner Like to Hear?: The best way to use words of affirmation is to know what your partner likes to hear. Your loved one might be more concerned about their contribution to the relationship than appearance. Or they might want you to acknowledge the things they do on a day-to-day basis, like go to the gym, cook dinner, or take the trash out. There is no one-size-fits-all when it comes to words of affirmation. You know your partner, and you will know what they like.

Be Creative: There is more than one way to say words of affirmation to your partner. Try thinking outside the box and get creative when speaking in their love language. You can do things like write a poem, a song, leave notes in places they will see them, leave a voice note. Your partner will really appreciate all the effort you put into making them feel special.

How to Ask Your Partner for Words of Affirmation

Communication is everything in a relationship, and your partner is not a mind reader. If you feel you are not getting what you need, you've got to ask for it. Here are some tips on how to do so:

Just Ask: Don't wait until you are frustrated and resentful before you bring up the issue. By brushing the situation under the rug, you are delaying your own happiness. I understand that people with an avoidant attachment style will find this difficult to do because burying their feelings is a coping mechanism. However, pushing through your fears is a part of the healing process, so take a deep breath and ask!

Have a Direct Conversation: Fishing for praise and compliments is highly annoying, and I am certain your partner will feel that way too. It makes you look desperate, and no one finds desperation attractive. Also, no one likes giving compliments when they feel it's being squeezed out of them. Basically, instead of using underhand tactics to get what you want, just sit down and have a direct conversation about it.

Be Mindful of Your Approach: When you have this conversation with your partner, be mindful of your approach. Remember, he/she is just as new to this as you are. They have no idea what they are doing. Think about it like this: When a person from a non-English-speaking country comes on vacation to America, you are not going to get annoyed with them because they can't communicate with you, you are going to help them out as much as possible, right? Use the same approach with your partner. Don't speak in an accusatory tone and say things like, "You don't make me feel special." A better way of saying it would be, "It would make me feel really special if you…" (we will discuss communication more in Chapter 9).

Give to Receive: I believe there are universal laws that activate what we need when they are applied. First and foremost, if you want your partner to praise you, you've got to give them something to praise you about. You can't expect praise for being a miserable nag who never has anything good to say. Also, put the same effort into speaking your partner's love language as you want them to put into yours. Your significant other is more likely to make an effort when they can see you are making one.

Date Night Challenge Words of Affirmation

The point of date night challenges is to make learning each other's love languages fun. You should do this no matter how long you've been dating. Not only will you get to know each other better, but you also get to spend quality time together. The challenge is called Popsicle Stick Affirmations, and this is how you play it:

Get ten popsicle sticks each and write the first part of an affirmation statement on each stick. You might write something like:

- I feel proud of you because...
- I appreciate you because...
- I feel loved because...

You want to create emotion here, and the best way to do this is to start with the words, "I feel [emotion]." Once they are all written up, put them in a cup. You can then pick them out and finish the sentences about each other over dinner or a glass of wine. However way you want to do it, just make sure you make an evening out of it.

Examples of words of affirmation include the following:

- I love you.
- Did I tell you how much I appreciate you?
- You mean everything to me.

- I just wanted to tell you that I'm proud of you.
- Your hair looks amazing like this.
- I love watching you take care of our kids.
- It makes me so happy when you make me laugh.
- You are more than capable of speaking at that event.
- I love the sparkle in your eyes when you are working on your passion.
- You did a fantastic job with this; tell me more about it.
- Thank you for making me feel loved and safe.
- I feel so blessed to have you in my life.
- What we've built is so beautiful.
- I think you are gorgeous.
- I love it when you smile. Your dimples are so cute.
- Thank you for being so loving and sweet to my friends and family.
- I appreciate that you do [insert] when you are tired.
- I love the way you always put 100 percent into everything.
- I am so grateful for the work you do around the house.

Acts of Service

At its core, acts of service are about demonstrations of love. For some people, actions speak louder than words. This is especially true if you've got a disorganized attachment style. You were hurt so badly in your childhood that words just don't mean anything to you. After the abuse, your parents always apologized and said it would never happen again. But it did, and so now, you have zero interest in hearing what people have got to say. According to clinical psychologist Dr. Beverly Palmer, people who are very ambitious and self-sufficient are also likely to have acts of service as their primary love language. If your partner wants to step in and make your life easier, that's what you consider real love. You are not really concerned about the act itself. What's important to you is that they are doing it because they are on your side.

If your partner makes the effort to pick your mother up from the airport or call the event planner so you don't have to, what you hear is, "I care about you, so I want to take on as much of your burdens as I can, even if it means sacrificing my own time."

Acts of Service When You Are in a Relationship

It's important to understand that acts of service can become a problem if you've got limited self-awareness.

Your relationship should be about balance, and as with all love languages, there is a chance that your expectations could get in the way of developing a healthy relationship. For example, even though you are super independent, in your mind, you might be thinking your partner should be doing certain things for you, and if they don't, you jump to the conclusion that it's because they don't love you. Or you start an argument or start acting cold. Basically, you can't expect your partner to help you out all the time, or you risk damaging the relationship. An unbalanced relationship where one partner expects too much makes things difficult, and your significant other will start feeling like you are too high maintenance. If you want the best for your relationship, here are some things to consider with the acts of service love language:

Your partner is not a mind reader, and there is no room for making assumptions here. Therefore, you will need to tell your partner what you value so they know how to give it to you. Again, remember it's all about balance. There is a fine line between telling your partner what you want and being too demanding. Here are a few tips:

- Be honest about the acts of service you value, and let your partner know why the things you want them to do mean a lot to you. For example, if you've been working overtime and getting home after midnight and you are the one who always walks the dog in the morning. You can ask your partner if they mind walking the dog so you can get an extra hour of sleep. Again, refrain from fishing for acts of service, especially if you are a woman. Fishing involves doing things like telling your boyfriend about all the nice things your friends and family do for you. Men don't respond to hints, so you've got to be straightforward with them. He might even take it the wrong way and assume you are trying to make him jealous, which will make him even more defensive.

- Once you've had your discussion about the acts of service you appreciate, pay attention to when they do them, and don't neglect to say thank you; first and foremost, it's the polite thing to do, and second, showing your appreciation lets your partner know you are not taking advantage of them. When you say thank you, make sure you tell your partner why you are grateful. For example, "I noticed you got my suits from the dry cleaners while I was at work. Thank you for that. I really needed them this week, and it would have been a nightmare trying to collect them with my current schedule."

- There are some things your partner won't be able to do, or they may not feel comfortable doing. Don't get upset or angry about it because your significant other isn't your paid personal assistant. When you hear the words, "Sorry, I can't do that right now," or, "I won't be able to do that until next week," accept it gracefully and move on, and trust that your partner would do it if they could. Remember, they've got their own life to live too. You should also bear in mind that a bad attitude won't give your partner any incentive to continue speaking in your love language.

Date-Night Challenge: Acts of Service

This game is called Jacks, Kings, and Queens of Service.

Props: A pack of playing cards, pen, and paper.

Write out three acts of service that need completing over the weekend. They could be taking the kids swimming, going grocery shopping, chores around the house, etc. Now assign one task to the jacks, kings, and queens. On the rest of the cards, write a quick act of service that you or your partner should perform. Shuffle the cards and put them in the middle of the table. Take turns in picking a card. When you get a quick act of service, you've got to perform it immediately. When you get a jack, king, or queen, put the card next to you. At the end of the game, total the number of jacks, kings, or queens you have. Whoever has the most has got to do the act of service assigned to that card. If you both have the same amount of any card, you've got to do the activity together.

Quick Service Ideas

- Stare into each other's eyes for 20 seconds
- Give each other a kiss
- Write a love note for your partner to read later
- Clean up something in the room you are in
- Look for a piece of candy or gum for your partner
- Tell your partner three things they've done today that you appreciate
- Brush your partner's hair for 20 seconds
- Get your partner a drink/snack

Examples of acts of service include the following:

- Take out the trash
- Take the dog for a walk
- Feed the cat
- Do the dishes
- Do the laundry
- Collect the mail
- Make breakfast, lunch, and dinner

Gift-Giving

If gift-giving is not your love language, you've probably rolled your eyes at this one. The misconception about this love language is that people who like receiving gifts are materialistic. But that is far from the truth; the receiver thrives on the effort, love, and thoughtfulness behind the gift. It lets them know that you are thinking about them, you care about them, and you want them to be happy. People who speak the love language of gift-giving get very excited about birthdays, anniversaries, and special occasions because of the buzz surrounding the gifts. Therefore, it's really important that you don't forget these dates or your partner will be heartbroken. You don't need to break the bank to be a gift-giver because it's often the smallest things that hold the most sentimental value for the receiver.

Gift-giving is actually the most widely performed act of love. No matter what culture or religious belief, people around the world give their friends, family, and loved ones gifts to show their appreciation and how much they care. An interesting fact I've found out about the word gift is that it originates from the Greek word *charis,* which means grace, and grace is unmerited favor. So when someone gives a gift from the heart, it is given out of a deep desire to demonstrate unconditional love and not as a way of getting into the receiver's good books.

Gift Giving When You Are in a Relationship

If gift-giving is your primary love language, you won't have any difficulty buying gifts for your partner because it's easier to tune into their energy since you speak the same language. But if this is not the case, you will find it challenging to communicate with your significant other with your gift-giving. For example, in general, people give gifts on birthdays, holidays, and special occasions. But your partner is likely to get very upset if you visit another state and return empty-handed. Your failure to buy a souvenir will be interpreted as you weren't thinking about them while you were away. The good news is that you can learn to speak your partner's love language. Here are a few tips:

- Pay close attention to your partner; listen out for things like their favorite color, their favorite chocolate, an item that they have been thinking about but haven't had the chance to buy yet. Make a list of these preferences and items as they are mentioned, and use the information to make your buying decision.

- As mentioned, don't think of gift-giving in terms of material value. If you are a millionaire, and you go out and buy your partner a brand-new Mercedes just because you felt like buying them a new car, you probably won't get the same response if you bought them the jigsaw puzzle they didn't get to finish when they were a teenager. They would really love to finish the puzzle, but it's not in stock anymore. The fact that you heard the desire in your partner's voice when they were telling you about the puzzle, and then you went out of your way to find it will mean a lot more to your significant other. To the person whose love language is gift-giving, something small and thoughtful screams "I love you" much louder than an expensive gift with no thought behind it.

- Get into the habit of gift-giving no matter what season the relationship is in. Outside of birthdays, special occasions, and holidays, some people only give gifts to get back in their partner's good books. I am not suggesting that you buy gifts for your partner every week but pay attention to the times when it would be appropriate.

Date-Night Challenge: Receiving Gifts

The challenge is to give your partner one gift a day for five days. Each day, give your partner something nice. I am going to break down each day and tell you what you should choose for your significant other. Don't worry about breaking the bank. Each gift costs less than $5, so you'll be fine!

Monday: Look for a gift that reminds your partner of your first date. You can get really creative with this. Let's say you took your partner bowling on the first date. You can make them a BOWL of their favorite soup! Get it? If you went to an ice cream parlor, get them the same flavor ice cream they ate that day.

Tuesday: Buy two gifts that describe how you feel about your partner. For example, if your girlfriend makes you laugh, get her a mug with someone smiling on it. If your boyfriend makes you feel warm inside, get him a mug with a picture of a fire on it.

Wednesday: For the third gift, surprise your partner with something that will simplify their life. If your boyfriend does a lot of work outside in the cold, buy him a pair of gloves. If your girlfriend practices yoga every day, get her a new stopwatch.

Thursday: Go out and buy your partner's favorite drink to have with dinner that evening.

Friday: Buy your partner a gift that has a strong connection to your relationship. For example, a picture of the country where you took your first vacation.

When you are the gift giver, you will need to look at things through a filter in your daily life. For example, if your partner likes donuts, you can no longer walk past the bakery and go home empty-handed. Or buy one for yourself to eat at the bus stop but also pick one up for your partner; they will be extremely grateful. Your partner might have a favorite childhood candy that's no longer sold in the stores. Search for it online and surprise them. If your boyfriend is a dog lover, buy him random items with dogs on them, like mugs and pens. Maybe your girlfriend enjoys a Starbucks coffee some mornings, so buy her a voucher.

Physical Touch

Physical touch is another love language with challenges. Women often complain that their partners want to go all the way after a quick hug and a kiss. When their advances are rejected, they get offended. Therefore, it's important to understand that when a person's love language is physical touch, it's not about sex all the time. It means that you receive love through physical expression. In general, physical touch is important because it triggers the brain to release the feel-good hormone oxytocin, says relationship coach and behavioral scientist Clarissa Silva. Physical touch in a relationship not only helps develop a strong bond but also boosts the immune system.

Physical Touch When You Are in a Relationship

Here are some examples of how to speak the language of physical touch when you are in a relationship:

Cuddling: Cuddle with your partner when you are lying in bed, watching a movie, or wrap your arms around him when he is folding the laundry. When you are together, find opportunities to cuddle each other.

Holding Hands: Hold your partner's hand when you are out in public or in private. It's a quick and easy gesture that immediately boosts feel-good hormones and strengthens your intimate connection.

Kissing: Kissing is often a form of foreplay, but it doesn't have to lead to sex if you don't want it to. You can kiss your partner on the forehead, cheek, ear, hand, lips, or neck. Where you kiss your partner is up to you. Just make sure it's soft and gentle.

Skin to Skin: Running your finger along your partner's back, rubbing the back of their neck, or placing your hand on their bare leg can be a way of letting your partner know you are present, you love them, and you are physically attracted to them.

Sitting Side to Side: Sitting close enough to your partner so you are touching is another way to express physical touch. You might be out at an event or out for dinner with friends and want to display affection without making others uncomfortable.

Tickling: Some people don't like being tickled, so if you know your partner doesn't like it, don't do it. But tickling can be a really fun way of incorporating physical touch into your relationship.

Finally, don't neglect physical touch just because you've had an argument and you are in a bad mood. You should definitely give each other some space to get your emotions together; however, resume physical touch as soon as possible because, as mentioned, all forms of physical touch release feel-good hormones, which will make it easier for you to forgive each other for your transgressions.

Date-Night Challenge: Physical Touch

Spending no more than $5, buy a packet of food coloring, a tub of frosting, and a roll of sugar cookie dough. On your date night, bake and decorate a giant cookie with each other. The rules of the game are that both of you can only use one hand. The frosting must be divided into three different bowls so you've got three colors. Once the cookie is ready, remove it from the oven, and then both decorate it with one hand each.

Take a picture of your completed challenge, and then eat it while watching a movie together.

Another game you can play is physi-golf. Create a mini-golf course in your house. You can either make the golf course yourself if you are good at improvising, or you can buy one from Amazon. With each hole, this is what you'll need to do:

- Put your hands around your partner's hips
- Softly blow on your partner's ear
- Slide your hand up your partner's back
- Massage your partner's shoulders
- Place your hand on top of theirs
- Hug your partner
- Put your hands over your partner's eyes

Decide how many rounds you want to play, and whoever loses has to make their partner a dessert.

Quality Time

All couples need to spend quality time together to strengthen their relationship. However, when your partner's love language is quality time, it will mean more to them than anything else. Does your partner get upset when you are having a conversation and flicking through your phone at the same time? They may even abandon the discussion and get up and walk off. Or they get really upset when you cancel a date even if you've given them plenty of advance warning. Unfortunately, most of us live in a fast-paced environment, and we are always on the go. We can be talking to someone face-to-face without being present, we are either going through our phones, or in our own heads thinking about our next move. This behavior does not go down well with people who speak the love language of quality time. They need their partner's undivided attention. They want you to turn off the laptop, put the device down, and focus on them. When you do, they feel loved, appreciated, special, and important.

Quality Time When You Are in a Relationship

As with all the other love languages, if you don't speak it, it will feel very unnatural to you. Especially if you are attached to your phone, or you are a naturally distracted person and break eye contact as soon as you think you've heard something suspicious. But with some practice, you will soon get used to it. Here are some tips on speaking the language of quality time:

Technology Boundaries: Nothing aggravates a person who speaks the language of quality time more than trying to share something with someone who isn't giving them their undivided attention. When you are with your partner during dinnertime, for a coffee break, or on a date night, put your phone away. I would advise putting it on silent or turning it off because the distraction from ringing and pinging is equally as annoying. It's best to look at your phone once quality time with your partner is over.

Active Listening: Active listening doesn't come naturally for most people. The reality is that, in general, humans are terrible listeners because as a person is speaking, we are thinking of a response and waiting for a chance to cut them off so we can butt in with our grandiose opinion. You can improve your active listening skills by doing the following when you are speaking to your partner:

- Unless they ask for it, don't give advice
- Lean in when they are speaking
- Pay attention to what they are saying
- Let them finish speaking before responding
- Be empathetic and think about how you would feel in their situation

Make Eye Contact: Eye contact is one of the most important aspects of quality time with your partner. Holding their gaze lets them know you are present and they've got your full attention. Making eye contact makes them feel loved, important, and understood. It is also another way of saying that you care about what they've got to say.

Quality is Everything: A person who speaks the love language of quality time isn't going to appreciate the fact that you've been with them all day but spent the majority of your time sending emails. When you don't understand this love language, as far as you're concerned, your presence is enough even if you are not paying them any attention. Your significant other would rather you spent an hour completely focused on them because, unfortunately, anything else is a waste of time.

Make a Plan: While it's great to be spontaneous, planning your quality time together in advance is a great way of making sure things run smoothly. This is especially true if you live an active life. When you block out time for your partner, it makes it easier to focus. You can make the most out of your quality time together by incorporating it into your daily routine. For example, you can spend time meditating, praying, reading together, or going to the gym together.

Date-Night Challenge: Quality Time

This is another weeklong challenge; every day, you've got to make space in your schedule and spend quality time with your partner. The rules of the challenge are that you will need to spend 45 minutes together. Here is a list of ideas, but obviously, you can also make up your own.

- Write a song about your relationship

- Go to the mall and go into the most expensive shops and pick a gift you would buy your partner if you could afford it
- Make homemade burgers and eat them while watching the sun set
- Sit outside in the dark and watch the stars
- Go for a drive
- Find a recipe you haven't tried before and make it together
- Do a DIY project together by completing a bit each day
- Plan where you are going to go on your next vacation
- Play a board game or do a puzzle together
- Go for a walk in the park

What is my Love Language? (Quiz)

After reading the above information, you may have already determined what your love language is, but if you are still not sure, the following love language quiz will let you know.

To find out your love language, go down the list of questions and tick the ones that apply to you. The love language with the most ticks is your love language; you may find that you get the same results for more than one love language. If that's the case, go through a process of elimination by ranking your answers in order of importance to find your secondary love language.

Quality Time

- You enjoy spending quality time with your partner, and you hate being interrupted. It's important to you that there are no distractions, and you get to bask in each other's presence and give each other your undivided attention.
- You feel special when your partner makes time for you, puts you first, and doesn't cancel the plans you've made together.
- Creating special moments and memories is very important to you. You love having new experiences together.
- You value time, and when you are together with your partner, you want to spend every second with them.
- You feel happy and content when you are around your partner, even if you are not doing anything.

Words of Affirmation

- You like it when your partner says, "I love you." These words are meaningful and special to you. The more they say it, the better you feel.

- You like your partner praising and acknowledging you; no matter how small the deed, you want to know that you are valued.

- You care about the details. It means a lot to you when your partner notices that you got your hair done, lost a bit of weight, or made an effort to dress up. To you, it shows that they are paying attention.

- You feel special when your partner takes the time to comment on something you have done.

- You like to hear your partner say, "Thank you," because it makes you feel affirmed and recognized.

Acts of Service

- You feel as if your partner wants to take care of you and release some of your burdens when they do things like the washing up or the laundry.

- You like it when your partner is paying attention to what you are doing and steps in to help at the right time. When they do things like this, you feel that they are paying attention to the small details, and it makes you trust them more.

- Words mean nothing to you until they are backed up by action. You need to know that you can rely on your partner and that they will be there for you when you need them.

- You like it when your partner steps in and does small things to make your life easier.
- When you are feeling tired and stressed out, you want your partner to notice without you having to tell them. Once they notice, you expect them to do something to make your life easier.

Touch

- You enjoy physical intimacy and look forward to hugs and kisses.
- When there is a strong physical connection in a relationship, you feel grounded.
- When you are out and about, you enjoy public displays of affection.
- You like sitting close to your partner. When they are near you, you automatically reach out to touch them.
- You feel loved and wanted by your partner during sexual intimacy.

Gifts

- When you receive a gift, you feel loved. It's not so much the present; you appreciate the thought behind it. The gift acts as a reminder that your partner was thinking about you.

- You like to take home memorabilia after a trip or a date because it reminds you of the precious time you spent with your partner.
- You like surprise gifts. It helps you build a deeper connection and strengthens the bond between you.
- You like receiving gifts and treasure the act of kindness.
- You like to honor occasions such as birthdays, holidays, and anniversaries with a gift. They are special days for you, and every time you see the gift, you are reminded of the event.

People Prefer Words of Affirmation

In 2010, Chapman evaluated the results of 10,000 people who took his quiz online and discovered that the most popular love language was words of affirmation. However, the dating app Hinge conducted a similar study and found that quality time was the most common love language.

I personally believe that love language preference depends on things such as culture, gender, values, and customs. For example, it is highly unlikely that words of affirmation would be the favorite love language in South Asian culture because they find direct praise very uncomfortable. I have a friend who comes from Ghana in West Africa, and public displays of affection are frowned upon, so there is a chance that physical touch won't be the most preferred love language there.

Now that you speak the same love language, the final step in overcoming relationship anxiety and rediscovering your love for each other is knowing how to resolve conflict effectively.

Chapter 8: Step 6: Effective Conflict Resolution Strategies

"Peace is not the absence of conflict, but the ability to cope with it." ~ Dorothy Thomas

There is no such thing as a perfect relationship; no matter how well you know each other or how much you love each other, conflict is going to arise at some stage. The question isn't if, but when. However, the difference between a good and a bad relationship is the ability to resolve conflict. Contrary to popular belief, anger can actually be a positive emotion if it's used in the right way. The problem is that most people don't know how to manage their emotions and react as soon as they feel hurt instead of processing the information and then responding in a rational manner. In Chapter 7, you learned all about speaking each other's love languages; that's great because you know how to tell each other that you love each other. But the final piece of the jigsaw is learning how to resolve conflict in a way that you both benefit from, and that will strengthen as opposed to weakening the relationship.

Stick to the Point

What happened yesterday, last week, or last month is irrelevant. When couples are arguing, they will often bring up incidents from the past, thinking that it bolsters their claims, but all it does is prolong the argument, and you end up going round in circles. Going back in time adds another layer of difficulty to the discussion, and it will confuse your partner. Stick to the issue at hand so that you can find a mutual understanding and solution.

Listen: Being present during a discussion is important; you and your partner both have the right to get your points across. However, listening carefully to what the other person is saying is essential to finding a resolution. As mentioned, people have a tendency to either interrupt the conversation or get so consumed in thinking about what they are going to say that they don't listen properly. You might be raging inside as you listen to your partner, but let them speak and pay attention to what they are saying. Once they have stopped speaking, repeat what they have said to ensure you heard them properly. This type of listening is referred to as active listening, and it gives your partner confidence that you want to hear what they've got to say. Additionally, it will give your significant other an incentive to listen to you when it's your turn to speak.

Be Empathetic: The last thing you want to do during a conflict is see things from your partner's point of view. This means having to evaluate yourself and accept the role you've played in the conflict. We all want to feel that we are being listened to and understood, and we will often overtalk to get our partner to see things our way. But when the conversation goes in this direction, no one feels heard or understood because you are both too focused on getting your points across. However, when you can step into your partner's shoes and make an effort to understand how they feel, you are one step closer to a viable resolution.

Constructive Criticism: Constructive criticism is the type you get at work when your boss wants to enhance your performance, so he/she lets you know where you are going wrong. But you will always notice that the conversation starts and ends with talking about your strong points, and the criticism comes in the middle. The purpose of this is basically to soften the blow. It's called a "negative sandwich." In general, no one likes hearing about their weak areas, but the reality is if they are not highlighted, you will never grow. So if you want to get your partner to change their behavior, start by telling them their good points, then go into the criticism and end with their good points. You will notice a massive improvement in the way your significant other responds to you.

Don't Take Criticism to Heart: As you have just read, criticism should be dressed in colorful, positive wording to lessen the blow. But sometimes, your partner is going to forget everything they've learned and hurl a load of insults at you. Your immediate reaction will be to bite back because they've broken the rules, so you might as well break them too. However, tit for tat is not the way forward here. Since you are the one being criticized, take the initiative to understand where your partner is coming from. If she screamed, "You are so damn lazy!" think about why she would say that. Maybe you are not doing enough around the house, and your girlfriend is tired of cleaning up after you. You can diffuse a situation very quickly by being the rational person. Think about it like this: The only thing that can put fire out is water; anything else will just add fuel to the fire and make it worse. The same is true in your relationship. If one of you is aggressive, one of you must commit to taking on the passive role.

Own Your Stuff: Taking responsibility for your actions is a strength, not a weakness. Admitting when you are wrong will improve your ability to communicate with your partner, and it will deepen your trust for each other. When your partner knows that you will self-reflect and admit when you've done something you shouldn't have, they are more likely to approach you instead of bottling things up. You will also find that when you own up to something, your partner will also admit the role they played in the conflict, and in this way, there is more chance of it being resolved.

Learn How to Compromise: The "my way or the highway" attitude can't work in a relationship. In order for your union to last, you've got to compromise. Compromise means none of you get exactly what you want, but you are satisfied enough to move forward. When you compromise, you are letting your partner know that you respect them enough to put your will to the side to make sure they are happy.

Take Time Out: Emotions are powerful, and it is not uncommon for couples to break up because of something said in the heat of the moment. It is perfectly normal to get angry and frustrated with your partner, especially if you live together. But it's not okay to lash out and say hurtful things to each other. Once words are released, you can't take them back. When you start feeling like you are going to have an emotional outburst, take a break. Go for a walk, a jog, or go into another room. Process your emotions and allow your feelings to settle down before having a conversation with your partner.

Assertive Communication

Assertiveness is often mistaken for aggression, but it is the balance between passivity and aggression. Assertive communication enables you to draw the required boundaries and get your needs met without pushing your partner away or allowing anger and resentment to find their way into your relationship. Assertiveness is how you lay your cards out on the table so that your significant other can decide how they are going to proceed with the situation. Assertive communication is a healthy way of communicating that allows others to feel respected, but it's something you've got to learn. Here are some tips:

State the Facts: When having a conversation with your partner about the behavior you want them to change, stick to the facts. Stay away from judgment and negative labels because that will immediately make your significant other defensive. For example:

Situation: Your partner is always late, and now they have turned up late for your work party.

Inappropriate: "You've got no respect! Why can't you ever be on time?"

Assertive Communication: "The party started at 7:30 p.m. It's now 9 p.m."

No matter how annoying the situation is, your partner might have a legitimate excuse for being late. When you accuse your partner of having "no respect" for being late, you've labeled the behavior when you don't know the facts. But by stating the facts without judgment, you give them an opportunity to explain themselves.

Don't Exaggerate or Judge: Using the same example as above, by exaggerating or judging, you add fuel to the fire and limit the chances of resolving the issue.

Inappropriate Response: "Now the party is ruined because you didn't get here on time."

Assertive Communication: "Now there is less time for you to meet my co-workers because the party ends at 9:30 p.m."

Tone of voice and body language matters in assertive communication. Make sure what and how you speak displays confidence. Don't slouch; relax and look them in the eye, and use a pleasant but firm tone.

Start with "I": Starting your sentences with the word "You..." makes what you are about to say sound like an attack or judgment. Your partner's guard will immediately go up, and you've set the stage for an argument. However, when you start your sentences with "I," the focus is put on how their behavior is affecting you and how you feel. Also, it lets your partner know that you are not blaming them and taking ownership of your feelings. Because the reality is that no one has the power to control the way you feel, you choose how you react to someone's behavior. In this way, you reduce the chances of your significant other becoming defensive, which means it's more likely that you can work towards a resolution. For example:

"You" Statement: "You need to quit leaving the dishes in the sink at night."

"I" Statement: "I don't feel comfortable seeing the dishes in the sink first thing in the morning."

Finally, think about assertive communication as a win-win situation by looking for ways you can both benefit from a situation. After you've laid everything out on the table, the last stage of the discussion should be to come up with a solution that works for both of you.

Things You Should Not do During an Argument

Arguments escalate because people don't know how to control their emotions. They react to how they are feeling at that particular moment, and it often ends in disaster. You can avoid having any more dramatic showdowns with your partner by not doing the following:

Avoid Conflict: People with an avoidant attachment style hate conflict. They would rather act as if the problem doesn't exist, or when the discussion starts getting heated, they walk away. Avoiding conflict is the worst thing you can do in a relationship because the tension builds up, and eventually, there is going to be a nasty confrontation. One of my partners had an avoidant attachment style, and we ended up breaking up because I spilled a cup of coffee on the rug... IN MY HOUSE! I didn't understand it at the time, but now I know that was the straw that broke the camel's back. We never had a disagreement. He would always agree to disagree, so he built up a lot of resentment. He screamed at me as if I had committed the most unforgivable sin! It's much better to address conflict as it arises. Obviously, choose your battles wisely but refrain from avoiding conflict.

Being Defensive: Defensive people refuse to accept they have done anything wrong and will not even entertain the idea that they may have contributed to the problem. A defensive attitude hurts your relationship because you are basically saying that everything that's wrong with your union is down to the other person. You refuse to look at the situation from an objective and empathetic standpoint, which makes it impossible to come to a resolution.

Mind Reading: Things like assuming your partner is holding back sex because they are tired or that your partner was late for your date because they don't care about the relationship is not a good idea. You are not a mind reader, so you can't start an argument based on what you think you know.

Refusing to Listen: One of the most disrespectful things you can do to your partner is refusing to listen to what they have to say. Now I'm not talking about putting two fingers in your ears and singing kumbaya at the top of your lungs. I mean interjecting before your partner has had the chance to finish their sentence, rolling your eyes, or shaking your head in disagreement.

Playing the Blame Game: Some people think admitting their weakness makes them less credible in some way. So instead, they point the finger at their partner or whoever else they can shift the blame onto.

Focusing on Winning: Your relationship is not a competition; you are supposed to be on the same team. If one or both of you is focused on winning all the time, you will never get past first base. Think about it like this: If the members of a basketball team were each focused on being the star of the game all the time, there would be no teamwork, and the team would never win. On the other hand, when each team member plays their role and works together to win the game, they significantly increase their chance of winning. Your relationship will have a greater chance of succeeding if you operate as a team and work through conflict together instead of trying to beat each other down.

Now, on to the good stuff...wink, wink!

Chapter 9: Step 7: How to Keep the Flame Burning

"The meeting of two personalities is like the contact of two chemical substances: if there is any reaction, both are transformed. ~ Carl Jung

One of the main reasons why relationships and marriages fail is because they take work. When you first meet someone you are attracted to, you can't get enough of each other because your hormones are all over the place. When you call each other, see each other, kiss each other, you get a dopamine rush. Everything feels so good, fresh, and new. But these intense feelings soon start to fade, coupled with the anxiety one or both of you are experiencing about the relationship. That feeling quickly disappears, and now you want out. But since you are reading this book, I can only assume that you want your relationship to work, and if that's the case, there are things you will need to do. Think about it like this...the man or woman on the front cover of the magazine with a six-pack didn't get the body of their dreams by thinking about it. They spent hours at the gym, changed their diet, and made a lot of sacrifices. A relationship is no different. You've arrived at the final chapter, you've implemented all the advice provided in steps 1–6, you've seen great improvements, but the final step is keeping that romance alive.

Keep the Passion Alive

I can look at a couple and immediately tell whether there is passion in the relationship or not. They may have had it at the start of their relationship, but now it's clearly gone. Passion is a sense of intimacy and connection. It's a special bond you share with your partner that only the two of you can understand, but it is an undeniable chemistry, and when you walk into a room, it's felt. I have no idea where you are in your relationship. If the passion has gone, these tips will bring it back, and if the passion is still there, these tips will help you maintain it:

Date Night: Do you remember when you first started dating? How exciting it was when you were getting ready, the indecision about what to wear, the butterflies in your stomach? Bring those days back by arranging a date night once a week, every two weeks, or once a month. Arrange it according to your schedule, but be consistent and make it special. You should both take it in turns to arrange the date, and it should be a surprise. Get dressed like you are going somewhere. Hold hands and act like teenagers going out on a first date. I do this with my husband once a month, and we both very much look forward to it. I would also advise that you go out instead of staying at home. It adds to the anticipation. Your home is a familiar space, and the aim is to create a new experience with every date.

Work on Yourself: Couples have a terrible habit of letting themselves go when they get comfortable. This is the worst thing you can do in a relationship. Putting on weight, dressing down every day, and making no effort to remain attractive to your partner is a recipe for disaster. Some of you may disagree, but it is a common complaint from men and women during counseling sessions that my partner let him/herself go. This is especially true if you made a significant effort at the beginning of the relationship, but now, you can't be bothered. Additionally, it's a misconception that men are the only ones concerned about looks. Women also want to be attracted to their partners, and if they are not, the relationship will become stale very quickly. Additionally, consider how you feel about yourself. Are you happy with what you see when you look in the mirror? Are there areas in your life you know you can improve upon? Start working on these things.

Keep Touch Alive: Let's get one thing straight: Physical intimacy isn't about sex. It's about expressing your attraction and desire for one another through touch. My first relationship was totally devoid of physical intimacy. We touched each other when we had sex, and that was about it. My partner didn't hug me, hold my hand, or kiss me. That just wasn't his thing. His excuse was that he was raised in a household where there was no affection, and he had no desire for it. As a result, he was extremely cold and disconnected. One of the many reasons for ending the relationship was that he couldn't understand how his lack of affection was hurting me, and he refused to seek professional help. For me, physical intimacy was absent from the beginning. But for some of you, the relationship may have started off with a lot of affection, and now its dwindled. Physical touch is an important part of passion. For men, you may recall me mentioning in Chapter 6 that a major complaint from women is that their partners only get affectionate with them when they want sex. And I know this to be true from personal experience. Well, I suggest that you are affectionate with your partner all the time. In this way, having sex becomes a lot easier. Additionally, I am in no way suggesting that you should only be affectionate because you have an ulterior motive. Affection is important. It makes your partner feel wanted and desirable, and it will deepen your connection with each other.

Make Sex a Priority: You would have gathered by now that relationships require compromise. Most women need to feel an emotional connection with their partner before they are comfortable having sex, but men express their emotions through sex. A lot of women complain that their partners want sex all the time, but it's more than the physical act of sex. What men crave is the emotional connection through sex. Think about it like this: How do you feel when you ask your partner if he loves you and he brushes you off? Rejected, right? That's how your partner feels when you brush him off when he wants sex. Now, let's get this straight...this is not about agreeing to sex every time he asks, because sometimes you are just not going to be in the mood. On nights like this, just let your partner know that it's not about him. You just don't feel like it because of x, y, and z.

One great way to compromise when it comes to your sex life is to have designated nights when you know you are going to have sex. As far as I'm concerned, the "sex should just happen" statement is an annoying myth that's very unrealistic. Sometimes, when it comes to intimacy, a couple can become like two ships passing each other in the middle of the night. Either one of you isn't in the mood, or you're both working late and too exhausted. But sex is a very important part of a relationship, and if it's abandoned for too long, it opens the door to relationship issues such as infidelity. When sex is part of the glue that holds your union together, it's not something you should "try" and work into your schedule if you have time. It deserves some respect and dedication. Here are some tips on how to schedule sex:

- **Pick a Day and Time:** There are several factors that go into having sex. Outside of date and time, you should also think about when you feel most mentally and emotionally engaged or turned on. I started scheduling sex with my husband because he preferred it in the middle of the night. I go to bed early, and we both have busy lives. We started scheduling sex in the afternoons and early evenings when our energy was at its highest.

- **Be Flexible About Intimacy:** Don't feel pressured to have sex all the time on your sex date because this is really about intimacy. It's about expressing your love towards each other through physical connection. Scheduled sex is also about creating a safe space where sex is a possibility if you are in the mood. So have a conversation about what to expect during that time and be open to compromise so you are both happy.

- **Enjoy the Anticipation:** When I talk about scheduled sex with friends, they look at me like

I've lost my mind. The assumption is that your sex life has become so dull and boring that you've been reduced to making appointments. You might feel the same as you're reading this, but I and other couples I know who practice this find it extremely exciting. It gives us time to get ready and prepare, time to think about different outfits, toys, and anything else you want to indulge in on that day.

Surprise Each Other: Men, do you remember when you were trying to woo your partner? You bought her flowers, chocolates, and took her out to nice restaurants, right? Women, do you remember when you were trying to get your partner to notice you? You wore your favorite perfume and always made sure you looked attractive? Don't stop because you are settled in your relationship now. Keep it up outside of date night. Surprise each other every once in a while, buy each other gifts, write each other love notes. Get creative and think about what you can do to surprise your partner.

Learn New Things Together: Another reason for relationship fatigue is boredom. I actually hate the term "settle down" because that's exactly what most people do. I did it, the majority of my friends did it, and people are not happy because of it. Just think about the word settle; it's a form of acceptance. This is the way my relationship is going to be, and I've just got to accept it. My parents settled; they had the most boring lives ever. They went to work, came home, had dinner, sat in front of the TV, and went to bed. They didn't go on dates, never bought each other gifts, they weren't affectionate. But I just thought it was normal. They are divorced now, and I'm not at all surprised. When my siblings and I got older and left home, they decided to go their separate ways. They only stayed together because of us. I am close to my parents, so we've had long discussions about this, and they both agree that they settled down and got bored with each other. They had no idea what it took to make a relationship work. It has only been through my journey of self-discovery, having therapy, and reading books that I've learned about how to make a relationship work.

Learning new things together will keep you on your toes. Not only will it give you something to get excited about, but learning new things will add another dimension to your relationship. You will have interesting things to talk about, and you can help each other improve the new skills you are learning. Here are a few suggestions on the new things you can learn together:

- Learn a new language
- Learn a new hobby
- Take a dance/cooking class
- Learn a new skill

I do this with my husband now. We go swimming together every Thursday. None of us could swim, and we both hated it, so we decided that we would give it a go. We love swimming now, we read books about the different techniques, and we enjoy the challenge that it gives us. We spend a lot of time talking about our swimming class, and it's really helped us explore each other in a different way.

Keep Your Independence

People with relationship anxiety tend to want to live in each other's pockets. They do everything together and don't spend a single moment apart. They are lovers and besties. On the surface, this sounds great, but beneath the surface, the reality is that one or both partners are co-dependent. One of the symptoms of relationship anxiety is co-dependency, and it is unhealthy on so many levels, but that's not what this section is about, so let's talk about why you need to keep your independence when you are in a relationship. There are several things that define a healthy relationship, and one of them is independence. Two independent people meet and decide they want to start a life together. Your bond should allow you to grow dependently and independently. We discussed earlier that people let themselves go in relationships. Well, one of the reasons is because they lose their independence. They get so comfortable that they stop investing in themselves. Anyway, if you feel like you and your partner have been spending too much time together, here are some tips on how you can become independent again.

Do Something Alone: Doing things together is great, and I discussed that earlier. However, doing things by yourself adds another element of spice to your relationship. It gives you and your partner the chance to teach each other something new. Once a week, get into the habit of doing something on your own. Take a yoga class, go to dinner with a friend or family member—you might even want to go and watch a movie by yourself. I started a pottery class. It's fabulous, and I still take that class today, and as you can imagine, my house is full of pots! My husband loves it when I bring home new pots or when I reach another level in the class. He is super proud of me when I get my certificates!

Have Friend Time: I was so guilty of this. Any time I got a boyfriend, I would abandon my friends. They called me out on it all the time, but I was so desperate to be in a relationship that I ignored them. I damaged a lot of my friendships because of this, so I personally know how important it is to maintain your friendships when you have a partner. Also, it gives you time to miss each other, to wonder what the other is getting up to with their friends. Plan a night out with friends at least once a month, spend time speaking to them on the phone, and you should even go on vacation together.

Keep Your Dreams Alive: We all have dreams, goals, and aspirations, but it is not uncommon for people to get into a relationship and abandon them. Achieving your dreams takes work, and when all your time is invested in your significant other, your dreams can quickly become a distant memory. You should want your partner to achieve their dreams and vice versa. You should both support each other. In order to turn your dreams into a reality, you will both need space to get things done. Your dreams are an important part of who you are. They give your life meaning and value. You will start resenting your partner if you give up your dreams, and then the relationship you imagined you would have doesn't happen.

Learn to Say and Accept No: "Can we go together?" Sometimes, asking to accompany your partner everywhere they go is simply unacceptable. You should be free to go and do whatever you want. That is the whole point of trusting each other. When you say no to your partner or your partner says no to you, none of you should get upset or offended about it. The conversation should go something like this:

"I'm going to be bored by myself. I would love to come out with you tonight. Can I please?"

"I have no problem with you coming out with me, but first, this is my agreed night out alone, and second, you wouldn't enjoy it anyway. We are going to be watching football, eating chips, and talking about guy stuff. There won't be any women there, so you will probably be more bored there than you will here."

"Okay, well, maybe I will give Janet a call and see if she wants to go and watch a movie."

"That's a good idea. Give me a call if you are going to be out late so that I don't worry."

"Okay, honey. Have a good time tonight."

That's a healthy way to deal with the situation without feelings getting hurt. In a situation like this, your partner isn't rejecting you because he doesn't want you to be there. You've got to stick to the rules; you have both agreed to spend time with your friends alone. That doesn't change because one of you doesn't want to be home alone. Being independent means you should be able to accept your partner's rejection with grace and vice versa.

And that's all, folks. Now... it's time to get to work!

Conclusion

"When you stop expecting people to be perfect, you can like them for who they are." ~ Donald Miller

Falling in love is the easiest part of a relationship because it just seems to happen. You meet, you start spending time together, and before you know it, love is in the air. It is preserving and staying in love that is the difficult part, and this is where most people fail because not only were they not expecting it, but they also simply don't know how to commit to a relationship. No one teaches us how to maintain a relationship. There is no class for it in high school. So it's the messages we are sent from our environment that gives us insight into what a healthy relationship should look like. As you have read, if you were raised in a household that led to you forming an insecure attachment style, there is a high chance you are going to end up in a dysfunctional relationship.

If you want a healthy relationship that stands the test of time, you've got to work for it. As with everything worth having in life, it takes dedication, commitment, and discipline. You can read every relationship self-help book ever written and see the best therapists in the world, but if you don't apply what you learn, you will never free yourself from the bondage of relationship anxiety.

A strong and secure romantic relationship can serve as a source of continuous happiness and support throughout the good and bad times of life. Research suggests that being in a committed relationship has several benefits, such as less stress and faster recovery from illness and surgery. A good relationship encourages healthy behaviors such as consuming a good diet, exercise, and no smoking. It also provides people with a sense of purpose and well-being, and it adds years to your life.

You are reading this book because your relationship is broken or on the verge of breaking down as a result of the anxiety one or both of you are experiencing. In general, most couples only focus on their relationship when they realize there's a problem preventing them from moving forward. Once the issues have been resolved, they revert back to living on autopilot and forget about the relationship again. But romantic relationships need ongoing commitment and attention for the relationship to flourish. I compare relationships like this to diets. A person who is not happy with their weight will go on an extreme diet to lose the weight before a special event such as a vacation or a wedding. After they've reached their weight loss goal and attended the event, they go back to their bad eating habits, and eventually, the weight returns. Diets don't keep the weight off, and neither do they keep you healthy. You've got to make healthy eating a way of life. In other words, if you want your relationship to withstand the test of time, you've got to work at it continuously.

The seven steps in this book should be revisited often. Find ways of incorporating them into your daily routine and keep working on them until they become a habit. I don't believe there is a cure for anxiety because no matter how in control of it we are, life is always going to present us with circumstances that will trigger anxiety. We fight it by how we choose to react to the situation, so everything we have learned are coping mechanisms. The more you put them into practice, the easier it will become to reside in a place of peace concerning your relationship.

My hope for you is that you will work so hard on your relationship that your efforts will show up in every area of your life. We often look at other couples and desire to have what they have and become the couple that everyone wishes they could be like.

I wish you every success in your journey to beat relationship anxiety and rediscover your love for each other!

Thank you

Before you go, I just wanted to say thank you for purchasing my book. I poured a ton of time into this book and shared a lot of my personal experiences and those of people I spoke to when compiling the book to show you that you're not alone in this, and a beautiful and fulfilling life where you can feel safe and free from abuse is within your grasp.

You just need to reach out and make it happen. Every journey, even one along the road to recovery, starts with a single step. This is your permission to take yours.

It's also a fantastic thought to me that you could have picked from dozens of other books on the same topic, but you took a chance and chose this one.

So, a HUGE thanks to you for getting this book and for reading all the way to the end.

Now I wanted to ask you for a small favor. Could you please consider posting a review on the platform? Your reviews are one of the easiest ways to support the work of independent authors, and it's incredible to go online and see all the amazing support this work has received. I love hearing from you, and hearing your feedback inspires me to write more in the future and helps me to identify what to do better and how to be the best writer I can.

This feedback will help me continue to write the type of books that will help you get the results you want. So if you enjoyed it, please let me know.

Also by Amy White

Digital Minimalism in Everyday Life: Overcome
Technology Addiction, Declutter Your Mind, and
Reclaim Your Freedom

How to Declutter Your Mind: Secrets to Stop
Overthinking, Relieve Anxiety, and Achieve Calmness
and Inner Peace

Beginning Zen Buddhism: Timeless Teachings to
Master Your Emotions, Reduce Stress and Anxiety, and
Achieve Inner Peace

Gaslighting Recovery Workbook: How to Recognize
Manipulation, Overcome Narcissistic Abuse, Let Go,
and Heal from Toxic Relationships

Empath Secrets: How to Awaken Your Superpower,
Protect Yourself Against Emotional Overload, and Live
an Empowered Life

References

Bradbury, T. N., & Karney, B. R. (2019). Intimate Relationships (Third ed.). W. W. Norton & Company.

Chapman, G. (2015). The 5 Love Languages: The Secret to Love that Lasts (Reprint ed.). Northfield Publishing.

Fugère, M. A., Leszczynski, J. P., & Cousins, A. J. (2014). The Social Psychology of Attraction and Romantic Relationships (2015th ed.). Red Globe Press.

Goldschneider, G., & Elffers, J. (2013). The Secret Language of Relationships: Your Complete Personology Guide to Any Relationship with Anyone (Reprint ed.). Avery.

Johnson, S. M. (2019). Attachment Theory in Practice: Emotionally Focused Therapy (EFT) with Individuals, Couples, and Families (1st ed.). The Guilford Press.

Kappas, J. G. (1999). Relationship Strategies : The E & P Attraction. Panorama Pub Co.

Pollack, J. (2020). Conflict Resolution Playbook: Practical Communication Skills for Preventing, Managing, and Resolving Conflict. Rockridge Press.

Richo, D., & Hendricks, K. (2002). How to Be an Adult in Relationships: The Five Keys to Mindful Loving (1st ed.). Shambhala.

Scott, S. J., & Davenport, B. (2018). Mindful Relationship Habits: 25 Practices for Couples to Enhance Intimacy, Nurture Closeness, and Grow a Deeper Connection. CreateSpace Independent Publishing Platform.

Willerton, J. (2010). The Psychology of Relationships (Macmillan Insights in Psychology series) (2010th ed.). Red Globe Press.

PhD, Y. L., & Alexander, B. (2014). The Chemistry Between Us: Love, Sex, and the Science of Attraction (Reprint ed.). Current.

Cpc, S. G. P. (2020). Love More, Fight Less: Communication Skills Every Couple Needs: A

Relationship Workbook for Couples (Workbook ed.). Zeitgeist.